1001
Incredible
Things to Do
on the
Internet

❮ Books Written by Ken Leebow ❯

1001 Incredible Things to Do on the Internet

1001 Incredible Things for Kids on the Internet

300 Incredible Things to Do on the Internet

300 More Incredible Things to Do on the Internet

300 Incredible Things for Kids on the Internet

300 Incredible Things for Sports Fans on the Internet

300 Incredible Things for Golfers on the Internet

300 Incredible Things for Travelers on the Internet

300 Incredible Things for Health, Fitness & Diet on the Internet

300 Incredible Things for Auto Racing Fans on the Internet

300 Incredible Things for Self-Help & Wellness on the Internet

300 Incredible Things to Learn on the Internet

300 Incredible Things for Home Improvement on the Internet

300 Incredible Things for Seniors on the Internet

300 Incredible Things for Pet Lovers on the Internet

300 Incredible Things for Women on the Internet

300 Incredible Things for Game Players on the Internet

America Online Web Site Directory
Where to Go for What You Need

To learn more about these titles, visit:
www.300INCREDIBLE.COM

1001
Incredible
Things to Do
on the
Internet

Ken Leebow

WARNER BOOKS

An AOL Time Warner Company

AUTHOR'S NOTE: Every effort has been made to make this book as complete and accurate as possible. The information is provided on an "as is" basis, and no warranty of merchantability or fitness for a particular purpose is implied. The author and 300INCREDIBLE.COM, LLC, shall assume neither liability nor responsibility to any person or entity with respect to any loss, damage or suitability of the Web sites contained in this book.

Copyright © 2001 by 300INCREDIBLE.COM, LLC
Cartoons © Randy Glasbergen: randy@glasbergen.com
All rights reserved.

Warner Books, Inc., 1271 Avenue of the Americas, New York, NY 10020.

Visit our Web site at www.twbookmark.com.

For information on Time Warner Trade Publishing's online publishing program,
visit www.ipublish.com.

 An AOL Time Warner Company

Printed in the United States of America

First Printing: October 2001

10 9 8 7 6 5 4 3 2 1

Library of Congress Cataloging-in-Publication Data
Leebow, Ken.
    1001 incredible things to do on the Internet / Ken Leebow.
      p. cm.
    Includes index.
      ISBN 0-446-67881-3
      1. Web sites—Directories. 2. Internet addresses—Directories. I. Title: One thousand
and one incredible things to do on the Internet. II. Title.

ZA4226 L44 2001
025.04—dc21   2001026493

Book design and text composition by Spinning Egg Design Group
Cover design by Diane Luger
Cover art by Randy Glasbergen

❮ Dedication ❯

To the love of knowledge, change, our future,

and the possibilities that the Internet holds for all

◀ Acknowledgments ▶

Putting a book together requires many expressions of
appreciation. I do this with great joy, as there are several
people who have played vital roles in the process:

• My wife, Denice, who has been patient with me while I have
spent untold hours on the Internet.

• My kids, Alissa and Josh, whom I love dearly and who have become
Internet aficionados.

• Paul Joffe and Janet Bolton of TBI Creative Services,
for keeping me focused.

• Mark Krasner and Janice Caselli for sharing my vision of
the Incredible Internet books and helping make it a reality.

• My good friend and mentor Lenny Barkan, who has helped push the vision to another level.

• The multitude of great people who have encouraged and assisted me via e-mail.

❮ Table of Contents ❯

◀ How to Use This Book ▶

Tremendous thought and research have gone into the writing of this book. What is the best way to use it? You may be familiar with some of the sites, however, you have probably never been to an overwhelming majority of them. Our recommendation is to use the book in any combination of the following ways:

- Scan the pages randomly, identify sites that intrigue you, and make sure you mark them.
- Read the Contents and become familiar with the subject areas covered.
- Read through the Index of Site Numbers and discover many subjects that you might need now or in the future.
- Make this book your resource guide to the Internet. When you need to find a particular type of information, refer to the subject areas covered.
- When you have leisure time, pick up the book and check out some of the sites. You'll find that the ones we take you to can lead to thousands of others that are also useful and incredible.

❮ Introduction ❯

To be incredible, a site must meet our vowel criteria: A, E, I, O, U. You'll find the sites in this book to be either ACTIVE, ENTERTAINING, INTERACTIVE, OBJECTIVE, or USEFUL. With over two billion Web pages, the Internet can be difficult to navigate. Our goal has been to filter out the clutter so you can spend your precious time productively. The Net is a huge encyclopedia, and we have organized this book in an A to Z format for you. Enjoy your journey as you discover the needles in the Internet haystack.

Ken Leebow
Leebow@300INCREDIBLE.COM
http://www.300INCREDIBLE.COM

"Do you MIND?!"

>> Advice & Opinions

1 Got a Question?

http://www.askme.com

http://www.exp.com

These experts will probably have the answer.

2 Second Opinion

http://www.allexperts.com

It's usually a good idea to get a second opinion. From the arts to women's issues, these folks will answer your questions.

3 There's No Such Thing . . .

http://live.looksmart.com

http://www.inforocket.com

http://www.keen.com

. . . as a dumb question, and these folks will answer yours quickly. These sites do charge a small fee.

4 Kids: Ask an Expert

http://www.askanexpert.com

Here's a kid-friendly site where questions can be answered.

5 Get Smart

http://www.selectsmart.com

This site will help you make decisions on such topics as politics, pets, health, food, and more.

6 Decision Time

http://www.personalogic.com

Need help making a decision? Let this site be your guide—animals, cars, electronics, travel, and more.

7 Get an Opinion

http://www.epinions.com
http://www.productopia.com

These sites have information on various products and services ranging from appliances to travel. If you need advice, get an opinion here.

8 What's Your Opinion?

http://www.gallup.com

Since 1935, Gallup has been polling opinions on just about every subject. I think that 99 percent of those who visit this site will enjoy it.

9 Op-Ed

http://www.blueagle.com
http://www.opinion-pages.org

You'll have access to hundreds of current editorials, opinions, commentaries, and columnists from many newspapers and magazines around the world.

10 Public Agenda

http://www.publicagenda.org

Public Agenda is a nonpartisan organization that addresses a wide range of issues through research and citizen education.

11 Think Tank

http://www.upi.com/corp/links/think.shtml

Unlimited ideas and possibilities come from these think tanks.

>> Animals & Wildlife

12 Animal Adventures

http://www.jackhanna.com

Kids and adults enjoy Jack Hanna's friendly and humorous animal adventures. Get to know Jack at his site.

13 World Wildlife Fund

http://www.worldwildlife.org

This is a beautiful site that will inform you about life on our planet and the unfortunate endangerment and extinction of certain animals.

14 Searching for Animals

http://www.animalsearch.net

This animal-specific search engine has listings from bears to zebras. Of course, you'll also find animals that are more appropriate to bring home as pets.

15 Free Willy

http://www.aquarium.org/keiko/index.htm

This is the Web site of Keiko (of *Free Willy* movie fame). At one time Keiko lived in a two-million-gallon aquarium. Now you can follow his worldwide travels.

>> Art

16 The Best of Art

http://www.artcyclopedia.com

Need to find information about a certain artist or a particular piece of art? This encyclopedia is a work of art in itself.

17 The Journal

http://www.artsjournal.com

Each day, Arts Journal combs through more than 180 English-language newspapers, magazines, and other publications that feature writing about arts and culture.

18 Art History

http://witcombe.sbc.edu/ARTHLinks.html

Art has a very rich history, and you can learn all about it here.

19 Art Appreciation

http://www.nga.gov

Art is alive and well at the National Gallery of Art. Go for a tour today.

20 ## Art on the Net

http://www.world-arts-resources.com

If it has to do with art, you'll find it here.

21 ## Egg-ceptional

http://www.webcom.com/24k/eggsculpture

The carving of eggshells is definitely one of the world's most delicate art forms. Visit this amazing egg sculpture gallery.

22 ## It's a Dog's World

http://www.bluedogart.com
http://www.wegmanworld.com

These two famous artists have a special way of presenting dogs. Enjoy their creativity here.

>> *Auctions*

23 ### Name Brand Auctions

http://www.ebay.com
http://auctions.amazon.com
http://auctions.yahoo.com

These are all excellent person-to-person auctions where you can buy and sell almost anything you want. Many people have used these auction sites to assist with their businesses.

24 ### Doggone Fun

http://www.auctionbeagle.com
http://www.auctionrover.com

Run over to these sites. They'll sniff out some great deals for you.

25   **Auction Watch**

http://www.auctionwatch.com
http://www.searchandfound.com

Everybody has the bidding bug, and everything seems to be for sale. Use these sites to get in on the auction action.

26   **I Trust You, But . . .**

http://www.tradenable.com

. . . let's use an escrow account for completing our auction transaction.

>> Audio

27   **RealAudio**

http://www.realaudio.com

One of the most exciting uses of the Internet is the ability to watch and listen to video and audio on the Net. RealAudio is a pioneer on the Internet frontier. Download this software today.

28   **Listen Up**

http://realguide.real.com
http://www.broadcast.com

There are literally thousands of things you can listen to on the Net using RealAudio. This is a good starting point.

29   **Look Up!**

http://www.dccomics.com/radio

It's a bird . . . it's a plane . . . it's Superman! Listen to the original radio broadcasts.

30 **Safe Listening**

http://www.broadcast.com/simuflite
http://www.policescanner.com/police.stm

Listen to live conversations between air traffic controllers and pilots. When you've heard enough of that, tune in to see what the police are up to.

>> *Automotive*

31 **What Does That Automobile Cost?**

http://www.edmunds.com
http://www.kbb.com

Finally, you can be on equal footing with car dealers. No doubt you will know even more about new and used cars than the salesperson does.

32 **Used Car Appraisal**

http://www.nadaguides.com

Want to know the value of a particular used car? Check out this handy online version of the *National Appraisal Guide*.

33 **Kick Them Tires**

http://carpoint.msn.com

It's a new world on the Internet. Microsoft offers detailed information about new and used cars.

34 **Autobytel**

http://www.autobytel.com

Yes, you can buy a car on the Net. Autobytel will match you with a local dealer and even promises you a great deal.

35 Cars Online

http://www.autoweb.com

http://www.carsdirect.com

Tired of dealing with car salesmen in the showroom? From the comfort of your keyboard, buy your next car online.

36 Auto Lease versus Purchase

http://www.smartmoney.com/autos

http://www.autosite.com/new/loanlse/calc.asp

http://cgi.money.com/cgi-bin/Money/cgi-java/leaseorbuy

Learn about car leasing and do calculations here before negotiating a lease.

37 Smart Lease

http://www.leasesource.com

http://www.leasetips.com

Arm yourself with all of the details before you lease a car.

38 Auto Financing

http://www.peoplefirst.com

When buying a car, explore your financing options with these people first.

39 Used Cars

http://www.autotrader.com

http://www.carfax.com

Buy or sell a used car online. AutoTrader has over one million cars listed. When you buy a used car, get the used car facts at Carfax.

40 **Fuel Economy**

http://www.fueleconomy.gov

How many miles to the gallon does your car get? Now you have the answers with a click of the mouse.

41 **Auto Safety**

http://www.crashtest.com
http://www.nhtsa.dot.gov

Auto safety is an important issue. Read and learn about crash tests and highway safety.

42 **Car Talk**

http://www.cartalk.com
http://www.autoshop-online.com

Tom, Ray, and Autoshop have great automobile information on the Net.

43 **Auto Recalls**

http://www.alldata.com

Has there been a recall for your car? This site will tell you the repair and recall record for most cars all the way back to 1960.

44 **Everything Automotive**

http://www.autopedia.com
http://www.jcwhitney.com
http://www.automobilemag.com

These sites will provide you with a comprehensive parts guide, an encyclopedia, and an auto magazine.

>> Books

45 **Wanna Buy a Book?**

http://www.amazon.com
http://www.bn.com

These are great sites on the Net, with book reviews, interviews, and more. Of course, you can also easily search for a particular book and purchase it.

46 **Best Price**

http://www.bestbookbuys.com
http://www.isbn.nu

Get the best deal you can when you buy a book. These sites search many online bookstores for you.

47 **Rare Books**

http://www.bibliofind.com

Looking for a rare book? Bibliofind has a search engine that contains over twenty million old, used, and rare books offered for sale.

48 *New York Times Book Review*

http://www.nytimes.com/books

Over fifty thousand books are reviewed at this site.

49 **Gutenberg Project**

http://www.gutenberg.net

If a book is in the public domain, it can probably be found in its entirety at the Gutenberg Project.

50 **Reading Is Fun**

http://www.bookspot.com

This is the place to explore many great resources related to reading.

51 **Book It!**

http://www.bookradio.com

If you like reading, then I'm sure you'll love listening to these author interviews.

52 **Celebrity Read**

http://www.gpl.lib.me.us/wrwind.htm

I don't know where they find the time, but these well-known people apparently manage to read plenty of good books.

>> *Browsers*

53 **Browser Watch**

http://browserwatch.internet.com

What's the latest with Internet browsers? Browse this site to find out.

54 **Tabbed Windows**

http://www.netcaptor.com

This browser—available to download free—looks and feels like Internet Explorer. Instead of having multiple windows and Web sites opened, this site creates a tab view for you.

55 Opera Browser

http://www.operasoftware.com

Sing it loud and clear: There is another browser available to surf the Net.

56 Get Plugged In

http://www.realaudio.com
http://www.shockwave.com
http://www.acrobat.com

Many Web sites offer features and functions that use the above programs to play music, show flashy Web pages, and open documents. If you want these capabilities on your computer, be sure to download the applications.

57 Cool Toolbar

http://www.hotbar.com

Your browser toolbar probably looks pretty boring. Spice it up at this site.

58 Guide Me, Alexa

http://www.alexa.com

Download Alexa and you will instantly be guided to great sites as you surf.

59 Smart Surfing

http://www.flyswat.com

There are no insects at this site, but you'll find a lot to buzz about. As you surf, Flyswat's software turns key words of text into live, clickable links that lead to related Web resources.

"I've grossed over two million dollars since I started advertising my business on the Internet!"

>> Business

60 ### Business Directory

http://www.business.com

This site claims to be "your guide to high-quality business Web sites," and it does have accurate and good business information, without overloading you.

61 ### Business Research

http://www.brint.com

Is research your thing? Go to Business Research in Information and Technology.

62 ### Business Information

http://www.infousa.com

Here's a site designed for small business owners, entrepreneurs, and sales and marketing executives, but everyone can find some good information here.

63 ### Business Search Engine

http://www.b2bscene.com

Here's a search engine with business people in mind.

64 Tools of the Trade

http://www.inc.com/tools

If you're in the business world, you will want to take advantage of *Inc.* magazine's business tools.

65 Business to Business

http://www.smarterwork.com

There's a lot of focus on business-to-business transactions on the Net. This site matches small businesses with vendors.

66 Franchise and More

http://www.bison1.com

Bison stands for Business International Sales and Opportunity Network. It has a great search engine to identify franchise opportunities.

67 Small Business Information

http://www.bizmove.com

Here is a resource of small business information that is packed with guidelines and tools to help successfully manage your business.

68 Let's Talk Business

http://www.biztalk.com
http://www.allbusiness.com
http://www.smallbusinessadvocate.com

Got a small business? These sites have a large amount of information for those who do.

69 Entrepreneurs Only

http://www.ltbn.com

http://www.entrepreneurmag.com

It seems like almost everyone is trying to be an entrepreneur. If you are, these sites will help you get where you need to go.

70 Everybody Sells

http://www.salesdoctors.com

The Sales Doctor has a lot of information for the sales professional.

71 The Small Business Association

http://www.sbaonline.sba.gov

The SBA has a tremendous amount of resource information for any business.

72 SIC Code Lookup

http://www.osha.gov/oshstats/sicser.html

Find the SIC classification for any business.

73 It's the Economy, Stupid

http://www.dismal.com

Though the site name is Dismal, there is lots of interesting economic data here.

74 Trade Shows

http://www.tscentral.com

http://www.tsnn.com

Use these sites to find the schedule and location of trade shows and professional events for just about any industry.

>> *Calendars & Time*

 ### Clocks, Counters, and Countdowns

http://www.panaga.com/clocks/clocks.htm

http://www.calendarhome.com

You'll be surprised how many of these are on the Net. You'll find both serious and fun items here.

 ### Calendars Can Be Fun

http://www.timeanddate.com

http://www.webexhibits.com/calendars

Here are a couple of sites that will teach you about time and calendars. You can also compute the time between dates, such as how many days until the birth of the baby.

 ### Calendar Land

http://www.calendarzone.com

All kinds of interesting calendars are shown here.

 ### Time Management

http://www.when.com

http://calendar.yahoo.com

The time has come to use calendars and "to do" lists on the Net. You can even display your schedule to people on the Web.

 ### What Time Is It?

http://www.timeticker.com

http://tycho.usno.navy.mil/what.html

http://www.globalmetric.com/time

You'll never ask that question again. These sites will tell you the exact time all over the world.

80 Time Capsule

http://www.dmarie.com/timecap

Celebrating someone's birthday? Bring this time capsule with you.

81 Remind Me, Please

http://www.lifeminders.com
http://www.candor.com/reminder

Are you forgetful about your commitments? These sites will be happy to help you remember.

>> Cameras

82 Cameras Around the World

http://www.earthcam.com
http://www.webcamsearch.com

Can't get away today? See views from cameras in locations all over the world.

83 Community Cameras

http://www.camcity.com

It's almost as good as being there. From interesting locations to the bizarre, you'll find various cameras spanning the globe.

84 Puppy and Kitten Watch

http://kids.discovery.com/KIDS/cams/pet.html

Visit puppy and kitten cam and view one of thousands of pets that can be adopted.

>> *Cartoons, Comedy & Fun*

85 ### The Cartoon Corner

http://www.cartooncorner.com

Learn how to draw cartoons, and also find kids' quizzes, stories, and more fun.

86 ### Link Me Up

http://www.cartoonlink.net
http://wsj.cartoonlink.com

Customize financial cartoons with your own name in them. You can even e-mail these to your friends.

87 ### Mail That 'Toon

http://www.toonogram.com

Choose a cartoon from here to be e-mailed to someone with a note from you.

88 ### E-Mail Cartoons

http://www.randomhouse.com/features/emailthisbook

Some people love to e-mail jokes. Here are some cartoons from *E-mail.This.Book!*

89 ### Cartoon Portal

http://www.cagle.com

Every cartoonist on the Net is listed here.

90 Politically Incorrect

http://www.callahanonline.com

No, not the TV show. If you are tired of politically correct views, look at John Callahan's cartoons.

91 Randy Glasbergen

http://www.glasbergen.com

Randy's cartoons are used in this book. Check out his site for more laughs.

92 Al Roker.com

http://www.roker.com

Whether you like Al's weather forecast or not, you may enjoy his daily cartoons.

93 Hang on, Snoopy

http://www.snoopy.com

See the gang from *Peanuts* comics here.

94 Comics Are Fun

http://www.comics.com

You'll find comics from *Adam* to *Zorro* here.

95 Disney Secrets

http://www.hiddenmickeys.org

Learn all kinds of interesting stuff you never knew about Disney.

96 Disney Online

http://www.disney.com
http://www.disneyblast.com
http://www.disneybooks.com

The folks from Disney obviously enjoy and believe in the Net. If you like Disney offline, no doubt you'll also enjoy it on the Net.

97 Unofficial Disney Guide

http://www.laughingplace.com

This isn't an official Disney site, but it might as well be called "everything you ever really needed to know about Disney."

98 Have You Heard the One About . . . ?

http://www.nolo.com/jokes/jokes.html

Everyone loves a good lawyer joke (except some of the lawyers themselves). Load up on a few for the next party you attend.

99 Meet the Joke Jester

http://shadow.ieor.berkeley.edu/humor

Get some great jokes that are geared especially to your taste. Rate a few with the jester, and he will continue to provide you with jokes that you enjoy.

>> Celebrities

100 Celebrity Almanac

http://www.celebrityalmanac.com

Photos, real names, birth and death dates, and much more can be found at this almanac.

101 Celebrities on the Web

http://www.starbuzz.com
http://www.celebrityweb.com
http://celebritysightings.alloy.com
http://www.celebrityemail.com

Admit it, you're a stargazer. On the Web, you can look for as long as you want, and no one will know you're watching.

102 Star Search

http://e.sleuth.com
http://www.celebhoo.com

If you're looking for celebrity news, check out this search engine and Web portal site that is neatly categorized.

103 Celebrity Search

http://www.celebsite.com

Type in a name and you'll be sure to find interesting stories and information about your favorite celeb.

104 Where Do the Stars . . .

http://www.seeing-stars.com

. . . dine, shop, live, and do other things? You'll know after you visit here.

105 Celebrity Offspring

http://www.celebnames.8m.com

What do celebrities name their kids? From A to Z, this site has the answer.

106 ## Celebrity Address Book

http://www.geocities.com/Hollywood/Hills/9842/mainframe.html

Where do over twelve thousand celebrities live? Go to this address and you'll find the answers.

107 ## They're Famous and . . .

http://www.forbes.com/people

. . . very rich. Check out the *Forbes* "Celebrity 100."

108 ## Did You Say Gossip?

http://www.gossipcentral.com

Get the latest on all your favorite celebrities.

109 ## Hollywood Stock Exchange

http://www.hsx.com

Play this FANtasy game by "investing" in your favorite celebrities as if they were stock shares.

110 ## Celebrities Dead or Alive

http://www.dpsinfo.com
http://www.wa-wd.com

Remember what's-his-name? He played in that movie with whatchamacallit. Wonder no more. The Dead People Server lists celebrities who are long dead, newly dead, or might plausibly be dead.

"I just joined a support group for Internet addicts. We meet every night from 7:00 until midnight on AOL."

>> *Chat*

111 Be My Buddy

http://www.aol.com/aim

Send an instant message to friends who are online. America Online's excellent Buddy List software is available to anyone on the Net.

112 Yack, Yack, Yack

http://www.yack.com

Do you like to yack? Here is the ultimate site on the Net for chat rooms on a wide variety of topics.

113 Let's Talk

http://www.talkcity.com

Check out the neighborhoods and move right into the one that suits your needs.

114 Can We Chat?

http://www.icq.com
http://chat.yahoo.com

Chatting has become very popular on the Net. Jump in at these sites.

>> *College*

115 Locate a College Online

http://www.ecola.com/college
http://www-net.com/univ/list.html
http://www.universities.com

If a college is online, you'll find it at these sites.

116 College Bound?

http://www.collegeboard.org
http://www.act.org

To apply to college you have to take one of these tests. Learn all about the SATs and ACTs.

117 Test Preparation

http://www.testprep.com
http://www.ets.org

You can't take the test without some preparation. Take a sample test online. There are also other helpful resources at these sites.

118 Let's Review

http://www.review.com/college

If college is on your mind, you will not want to miss the Princeton Review.

119 College Rankings

http://www.usnews.com/usnews/edu/college/corank.htm
http://www.ope.ed.gov/security

U.S. News & World Report is well known for its annual college rankings. Learn about the rankings and much more at this site. While you're reviewing rankings, it's probably a good idea to review crime statistics reported by the U.S. Department of Education.

120 **Go College**

http://www.gocollege.com

It's hard to list all of the great things at this site. All I can say is, "Go there."

121 **Apply Online**

http://www.collegenet.com

Many colleges allow you to apply online. It's cool, easy, and fun.

122 **College Is Necessary**

http://www.collegeispossible.org

If you're thinking about college, you probably have some questions. This site has the answers.

123 **The Center for All Collegiate Information**

http://www.collegiate.net/infoi.html

This site merges the college and online worlds and offers a ton of information.

124 **College Newspapers Online**

http://www.all-links.com/newscentral/college

Cuddle up to your computer monitor and read a college newspaper. This can be a good way to get acquainted with a school.

125 **College News**

http://www.uwire.com

A Northwestern student started this publication in 1994. Now it is considered a premier news source for college life. Learn about the issues on campus.

126 What's It Gonna Cost?

http://www.salliemae.com/calculators/index.html

Let Sallie Mae help you with understanding the cost of going to college.

127 Financial Aid

http://www.finaid.org

Going to college? Want financial aid information? This is the "Smart Student Guide to Financial Aid."

128 Scholarships for All

http://www.fastweb.com

This is a great scholarship search engine. You'll find programs based on information you enter about your interests, experiences, and family background.

129 All Aboard

http://www.embark.com

Embark has everything you need to prepare for college and your future. The site offers a college search tool, useful links, advice, and guidance from an expert college panel.

130 You're Wired!

http://www.wiredcolleges.com

Learn about the most wired (Internet-friendly) colleges, and find a lot of other useful college and technology information at this site.

131 College

http://www.collegeview.com
http://www.campustours.com
http://www.collegequest.com

Take a tour of over 3,500 colleges and universities, and discover other goodies for the college-bound.

Buy the Book

http://www.varsitybooks.com

You'll be buying a lot of books while you're in college. Online there are no lines. There's even an "After Class" section, so go have some fun.

"Our palm-top computer is available with many options, including the nose-top printer, scanner hat, and 100MB removable storage socks!"

>> *Computers & Software*

 Computer History

http://www.computerhistory.org

Though computers have dramatically changed our lives, they have not really been around for that long. Learn about the history of computers from 1945 to the present.

 Help Me, Please!

http://www.pcsupport.com

As computers have become more sophisticated, good support has never been more vital. Use this site to get help for your hardware and software problems.

 Computer Assistance

http://www.protonic.com

The answers to computer and software questions are just a click away.

136   Consult the Digital Goddess

http://www.komando.com

Kim Komando, self-proclaimed Digital Goddess, will assist with your computer and Internet concerns. She has a national radio show, a newsletter, and many tips at her Web site.

137   Neat Net Tricks

http://www.neatnettricks.com

Subscribe to this cool newsletter and you'll receive tips about using the Net and your computer.

138   Learn to Type

http://www.learn2type.com

Typing has become an important skill for anyone who uses a computer. Test your skills here.

139   Keyboarding

http://www.absurd.org/jb/typodrome

How are your keystrokes? Take a few minutes and practice your keyboarding skills.

140   I Got a Virus

http://www.mcafee.com
http://www.norton.com

If you want to know more about viruses and how to get them out of your computer, visit these sites.

141   Screensavers and Wallpaper

http://www.webshots.com

Download these stunning enhancements for your computer monitor.

142 Shareware for Everyone

http://www.shareware.com
http://www.jumbo.com
http://www.download.com

Take a look at these sites to choose from millions of software programs to download.

143 Entertainment Software Ratings Board

http://www.esrb.com

Check out the ratings for software games here. It will also tell you specific age groups that contain the most appropriate players.

144 SuperKids

http://www.superkids.com

Get unbiased reviews of children's software by parents, teachers, and kids. There's also a humor section and other cool stuff at this site.

145 Searching for Software

http://tukids.tucows.com

Download virus-free educational software from this fun, safe site.

146 Software Version Tracker

http://www.versiontracker.com
http://updates.cnet.com

These straightforward sites tell you the current versions of many software titles.

147 Versions

http://www.versions.com

Do you need to know when a new version is released for a software product that you use? Versions will e-mail you when an update of your favorite software is available.

148 Computer Shopper

http://shopper.cnet.com

This indexes over four hundred thousand entries from computer cyberstores, so you can easily find up-to-date computer prices.

149 Buydirect.com

http://www.buydirect.com

Here is a very convenient location for purchasing and downloading software. Most of the leading software applications are available here at manufacturer's prices.

>> Consumer Issues

150 Consumer Issues

http://www.consumerworld.org

An amazing array of sites (over two thousand) will help you with consumer-oriented issues at ConsumerWorld.

151 Consumer Search

http://www.consumersearch.com

This site searches consumer reviews so you don't have to. Almost any product available has been reviewed here.

152 Consumer Reports

http://www.consumerreports.org

This world-renowned publication has been providing objective assistance to millions offline, and now has a wealth of information online.

153 Complaint Central

http://www.ecomplaints.com

http://www.planetfeedback.com

Have you had a problem with a company? Go to these sites and tell the world all about it.

154 Product Reviews

http://www.productreviewnet.com

http://www.consumerreview.com

Type in a category and find out about the product.

155 Recalls on the Net

http://www.safetyalerts.com

http://www.recalls.org

Make sure you're safe. These sites provide safety alerts and recall notices for all types of products.

156 Postal Inspectors

http://www.framed.usps.com/postalinspectors

If you're looking for information about mail fraud or want to report suspected mail fraud, this is the place to turn. You'll find answers to frequently asked questions, consumer fraud alerts, and a mail fraud report form.

157 National Fraud Information Center

http://www.fraud.org

This is an excellent antifraud resource containing concise information on fraud against the elderly, Internet fraud, telemarketing fraud, and more.

Can I Help?

> http://www.helping.org
> http://www.allcharities.com
> http://www.givespot.com

> Donate your time or money to a worthy cause. These sites list many organizations that could use your assistance.

 'Tis the Season

> http://www.sidewalksanta.org
> http://www.toysfortots.org

> It's better to give than receive. Have some fun and learn about these charitable organizations.

>> Crime & Conspiracies

 All Points Bulletin

> http://www.apbnews.com

> Do you like watching your local evening news? If you do, you'll enjoy this site devoted exclusively to crime, justice, and safety.

 Wanted!

> http://www.fbi.gov/mostwant/topten/tenlist.htm
> http://www.amw.com
> http://www.mostwanted.org

> Here are the lists of the FBI's Ten Most Wanted, America's Most Wanted, and the World's Most Wanted.

162 Sixty Greatest Conspiracies

http://www.conspire.com
http://www.jfk.org

Read about the "Sixty Greatest Conspiracy Theories." While you're at it, visit the Museum at Dealey Plaza, which chronicles the JFK assassination and legacy.

>> Dictionaries

163 Dictionaries

http://www.m-w.com
http://www.dictionary.com

The well-known Webster's dictionary is on the Net and even has a "word for the day" section. These dictionaries are actually fun and have a variety of other resources.

164 A Web of . . .

http://www.yourdictionary.com

. . . online dictionaries can be found here.

165 How's Your Vocabulary?

http://www.voycabulary.com

This amazing tool will link every major word at a given Web site to a dictionary or thesaurus.

166 Tough Words

http://www.lineone.net/dictionaryof/difficultwords

Search the Hutchinson Dictionary of Difficult Words index of over thirteen thousand entries to increase your vocabulary or just to find out what they mean.

167 **One Look**

http://www.onelook.com

You will, no doubt, look at this site more than once. It has over six hundred excellent dictionaries for different disciplines. Check it out on the Net.

168 **A, B, C . . . Z**

http://www.enchantedlearning.com/Dictionary.html
http://www.littleexplorers.com/Letters.html

These are fun dictionaries for the young members of the family. They present an engaging learning experience for the parent and child.

169 **Technology Dictionary**

http://www.whatis.com
http://www.computeruser.com/resources/dictionary/dictionary.html

Find out about words, emoticons, country domain names, and HTML stuff.

170 **Thesaurus**

http://www.thesaurus.com

It may sound like some kind of dinosaur, but Roget's is online for your assistance.

171 **3D Thesaurus**

http://www.visualthesaurus.com

Type in a word and then click on the words that are displayed. Follow the thread of meaning and create a spatial map of linguistic associations. Try it, it's really cool.

>> *Documents, Statistics & Lists*

172 **Document This**

http://www.lib.umich.edu/libhome/Documents.center/
webdirec.html

The University of Michigan has an A to Z listing of documents and Web sites. Spend a rainy day here.

173 **Core Documents of the USA**

http://www.access.gpo.gov/su_docs/dpos/coredocs.html

From the Bill of Rights to Supreme Court decisions, you can find it all here.

174 **List Mania**

http://www.statejobs.com/list.html
http://gwis2.circ.gwu.edu/~gprice/listof.htm

Do you love lists? You'll find plenty at this site.

175 **Statistical Rolodex**

http://www.cdc.gov/nchs/fastats

The National Center for Health Statistics provides a comprehensive index of interesting information.

176 **Internet Stats**

http://www.statmarket.com
http://www.mediametrix.com

These sites keep track of the growth, trends, and current news about the Net.

(177) Internet Demographics

http://www.cyberatlas.com

There is not really a great "handle" on demographics on the Net, but CyberAtlas attempts to give us some indication of what is happening.

(178) Got a Statistical Question?

http://www.internetstats.com

The folks at this site will search for almost any statistic for you. Just ask them to look for it, and if it's on the Net, they'll find it.

>> E-Commerce

(179) There's Gold Out There

http://www.strikingitrich.com

Everyone is wondering how to make money on the Net. Based on a book, this site discusses some Web sites that have done very well.

(180) Powerful Rankings

http://www.gomezadvisors.com
http://powerrankings.forrester.com

Gomez and Forrester rank and rate some of the various categories on the Net: travel, stockbrokers, autos, and other retail e-commerce sites.

It's an E-World

http://www.time.com/time/poy2000/archive/1999.html
http://www.ecommercetimes.com
http://www.zdnet.com/enterprise/e-business/bphome
http://www.nytimes.com/library/tech/99/09/biztech/technology

Everyone's talking about e-commerce, and these sites offer in-depth information, including Amazon.com's Jeff Bezos, *TIME* magazine's 1999 Person of the Year.

From $2,100 to $0

http://www.creativegood.com

Here's an offer that seems too good to be true. Creative Good provides a seventy-five-page report about e-commerce for free. Normally, this report sells for $2,100, so visit the site before the deal goes away. You'll find many other goodies here.

"Thank you for calling. Please leave a message. In case I forget to check my messages, please send your message as an audio file to my e-mail, then send me a fax to remind me to check my e-mail, then call me back to remind me to check my fax."

>> E-Mail & Newsgroups

 ### Free E-Mail

http://www.emailaddresses.com

You'll find listings for free e-mail services, articles about free e-mail, and resources to help you locate the e-mail addresses of family or friends.

(184) Vanity E-Mail

http://www.mailbank.com

http://www.iname.com

These sites have an incredible amount of e-mail addresses. So if you are not satisfied with the one you have, check it out.

(185) Autoresponder

http://www.mailback.com

Autoresponders are kind of like "Fax on Demand" but are easier to use and much more powerful. This site allows you to set up an autoresponder.

(186) Fax to E-Mail; E-Mail to Fax

http://www.faxaway.com

Learn how to send a fax to someone's e-mail or an e-mail to someone's fax machine. You can send it anywhere in the world.

(187) Fax and Voice Mail

http://www.efax.com

http://www.j2.com

Send a fax on the Net; it's so simple. You can even fax someone a word processing file.

(188) FIGlet

http://st-www.cs.uiuc.edu/users/chai/figlet.html

If you've never heard of FIGlet, go have some fun making interesting large letters out of ordinary text in your e-mail.

189 Liven Up Your E-Mail

http://users.inetw.net/~mullen/ascii.htm

http://www.ascii-art.com

ASCII art has been around for a long time. Enjoy the designs by these computer geeks.

190 Signature Tag Lines

http://www.mcs.brandonu.ca/~ennsnr/Tags/Welcome.html

Need a clever tag line for an e-mail signature? Choose from over 290,000 possibilities here.

191 DejaNews

http://groups.google.com

If you need to find something in a newsgroup, this is your place to go.

192 E-Mail Discussion Group

http://www.liszt.com

http://groups.yahoo.com

Want to communicate by e-mail with someone about a specific topic? You can do it here.

"Does anybody use the computers at your high school? I accidentally e-mailed them your diary."

>> Education & Schools

193 Search Education Sites

http://www.searchedu.com

There are over twenty million university and education pages indexed and ranked in order of popularity.

194 AskERIC

http://ericir.syr.edu

ERIC actually stands for Educational Resources Information Center. This federally funded national information system provides services and products on a broad range of education-related issues.

195 Schools on the Net

http://web66.coled.umn.edu/schools.html

What schools are on the Net? Web66 will surely let you know.

196 The School Report

http://www.theschoolreport.com
http://measuringup2000.highereducation.org

An amazing source for statistical information about each state and SAT scores by school, these sites also have maps and other information about each school.

197 ## National PTA

http://www.pta.org

You have probably been paying the dues for years. So visit the site and use the PTA's resources.

198 ## Turner, IBM, and Education

http://www.solutions.ibm.com/k12
http://learning.turner.com

Turner and IBM have interesting educational sites for grades K–12.

199 ## Education with Newspapers

http://education.usatoday.com
http://www.nytimes.com/learning
http://www.nytimes.com/library/tech/reference/linkseducation.html
http://www.nytimes.com/library/tech/reference/indexeducation.html

These two famous papers have sites dedicated to education. Teachers and students will find timely information.

200 ## FYI

http://fyi.cnn.com

CNN has created a Web site that is designed just for students and teachers. It's a great way to bring current events to the classroom.

201 ## *Newsweek*

http://school.newsweek.com

This special edition of *Newsweek* is designed to help teachers build bridges to real-world issues.

Family Education

http://www.familyeducation.com

This site is dedicated to helping parents take an active role in their kids' education.

"You've been working awfully hard lately. If you need a little fresh air and sunshine, you can go to www.fresh-air-and-sunshine.com."

>> Employment

 Looking for a Job?

http://www.monster.com
http://www.careermosaic.com
http://www.jobdirect.com
http://careers.yahoo.com

At these sites, you can search for a particular position, post a résumé, and learn about other ways to use the Net for job hunting.

 Need a Job?

http://www.hotjobs.com
http://www.careerbuilder.com

Seeking a career change? These sites will help lead you to greener pastures.

205 **The Search Is On**

http://www.jobsleuth.com
http://www.jobsearchpro.com
http://www.myjobsearch.com

Use these sleuths and search engines to make your career search easier. You'll find many tools to help with this important process.

206 **Job Portal**

http://www.employmentspot.com
http://www.rileyguide.com
http://www.jobhuntersbible.com

These sites will help lead you to an amazing array of job-related sites and information.

207 **Peek into the Vault**

http://www.vault.com

If you want information directly "from the horse's mouth," visit the Vault's Electronic Watercooler.

>> Encyclopedias

208 **Encyclopedias Online**

http://www.britannica.com
http://www.funkandwagnalls.com

Remember the old days of encyclopedias—twenty volumes and tons of information? The information is still there, but now it's online.

Encyclopedia.com

http://www.encyclopedia.com
http://encarta.msn.com
http://www.bartleby.com/65

Here are some well-known encyclopedias to assist with
your research.

 ### Encyclopedia Internet

http://www.cs.uh.edu/~clifton/micro.a.html

The Net is like a giant encyclopedia, but it is not categorized as
such. This is no easy task, but here is a site that does a good job.

 ### Information, Please

http://www.infoplease.com

The folks at Infoplease have great information in many categories.
You are sure to find something special and interesting.

When Pinocchio talks to girls online . . .

>> Entertainment

 ### Screen It!

http://www.screenit.com

Find out in advance what to expect from a movie, video, or DVD
that your kids want to see or buy.

213 **That's Show Business**

http://www.mrshowbiz.com
http://www.eonline.com
http://www.etonline.com
http://www.pagesix.com

No doubt, these sites will keep you entertained.

214 **Entertainment Online**

http://www.ew.com
http://www.fametracker.com
http://www.hollywood.com
http://www.showbizdata.com
http://www.hollywoodreporter.com

Entertainment begins here.

215 **Ticketmaster**

http://www.ticketmaster.com

Go here if you need tickets or a seating chart for just about any event.

>> Events

216 **It's Happening Here**

http://guide.yahoo.com
http://www.whatsgoingon.com

Go to Event Calendar and find out what is going on. You will be able to search by city, state, or venue. There are over five hundred thousand events in the database.

Join the Festivities

http://www.festivals.com
http://www.festivalfinder.com

From art to sports, you'll have fun researching these festivals.

 Culture Vulture

http://www.culturefinder.com

If you are in the upper crust of society, by all means check out CultureFinder. You can search for all those cultural events.

 RSVP, Please

http://www.evite.com
http://www.seeuthere.com

Are you having a party? Use one of these sites to invite your guests.

"Do you, Jason, take Heather to have and to hold, to e-mail and to fax, to page and to beep, until death do you part?"

>> *Family*

 Having a Baby

http://www.childbirth.org
http://www.babyzone.com
http://www.babysoon.com

Get ready for the roller-coaster ride of parenthood.

221 Having My Baby

http://www.pregnancycalendar.com
http://www.first9months.com

The Interactive Pregnancy Calendar will build you a day-by-day customized calendar that details the development of a baby from preconception to birth.

222 Name That Baby

http://www.babynamer.com

With over twenty thousand names in its database, you'll be sure to find the right name.

223 The Name Game

http://www.zelo.com/firstnames/index.asp

What does your name mean? Type it in and you'll instantly learn its origin and meaning.

224 Tell the World

http://www.softgreetings.com

Send an e-announcement to tell the world about your wonderful new addition.

225 Parent Portal

http://www.abcparenting.com
http://www.parentgarden.com

Whatever the issue, these portal sites will try to address it.

226 **Parent Soup**

http://www.parentsoup.com

All parents have been in hot water. Let Parent Soup bail you out.

227 **Parent Time**

http://www.parenttime.com

Parenting is never easy; let Parent Time assist.

228 **Parent's Place**

http://www.parentsplace.com

This site says, "We operate under the belief that parents are the best resource for other parents."

229 **House Calls?**

http://www.drgreene.com

Dr. Greene provides some pediatric wisdom for the information age. From prenatal to adolescents, this high-tech doc has it covered.

230 **Attention Deficit (Hyperactivity) Disorder**

http://www.oneaddplace.com
http://www.med.nyu.edu/Psych/addc/addctr.html
http://www.chadd.org

Need to know more about ADD? Check out some great resources at these sites.

231 **Surviving Your Child's Teen Years**

http://www.parentingteens.com
http://www.parentingadolescents.com
http://www.parenting-qa.com/teens.html

Remember, you also went through the teen years. Too bad there was no Internet to help your parents!

232 **Heeeelp!**

http://www.disciplinehelp.com

If you need a little help with your child, go to this site for over one hundred tips.

233 **Can We Talk?**

http://www.talkingwithkids.org

No one ever said parenting would be easy. Use this site's "ten tips for talking with kids about tough issues" as a starting point.

234 **Love Gone Bad**

http://www.divorcenet.com
http://www.divorcesource.com
http://www.divorcesupport.com

There's a lot of love talk on the Net, but the truth is that over 50 percent of the U.S. population gets divorced.

235 **Gather 'Round the Net**

http://www.myfamily.com
http://www.familypoint.com

In the old days, we gathered around the TV. Now you can have your family members gather around this Web site. You can chat, store pictures, maintain a calendar, and do other fun and creative things.

236 **Grandparents Online**

http://www.igrandparents.com
http://www.egrandparents.com
http://www.grandsplace.com

Get insightful news, useful health tips, shopping information, and more, all designed especially with grandparents in mind.

>> *Fashion*

 237 **Fashion and Style**

http://www.firstview.com

http://www.fashionmall.com

If fashion is your passion, these sites are for you.

238 **Designers Galore**

http://www.fashionlive.com

Be in style. You'll find the major designers and all the latest fashions here.

239 **It's All about Fashion**

http://fashion.about.com

From head to toe, this site has the world of fashion completely covered.

240 **I'll Wear That**

http://www.asseenin.com

If you want to emulate your favorite celebrities, this site is for you. Find out what the people you admire wear and drive.

>> *Financial, Corporate*

 241 **Meet EDGAR**

http://www.sec.gov/edgarhp.htm

The Electronic Data Gathering, Analysis and Retrieval system performs automated collection, validation, indexing, acceptance, and forwarding of submissions by companies and others who are required by law to file with the U.S. Securities and Exchange Commission.

242   He's a 10K Wizard

http://www.10kwizard.com

The 10K Wizard's market-leading, proprietary search technology lets users view SEC filings of more than 68,000 companies and search historical filings by key words, phrases, and names.

243   Corporate Report Card

http://www.prars.com
http://wsj.ar.wilink.com

Looking for an annual report on any one of 3,600 corporations? This is your site.

244   Corporate Knowledge

http://www.corporateinformation.com
http://www.companysleuth.com

Everyone is talking about the stock market. These sites will help you become a very knowledgeable participant. Get early earnings reports, listen to conference calls, and obtain lots of other corporate information here.

245   Companies Online

http://www.companiesonline.com

Get information on over five hundred thousand companies.

246   The *Fortune* 500

http://www.fortune.com/fortune/fortune500

This famous index of powerful companies currently lists General Motors in the number one spot at $189 billion.

247 The *Inc.* 500

http://www.inc.com/500

This is the *Inc.* magazine annual list of the five hundred fastest-growing companies.

>> Financial, Personal

248 How's Your Credit?

http://www.qspace.com
http://www.equifax.lycos.com

Obtain your personal credit rating, and find other useful financial tools here.

249 Credit Cards

http://www.cardweb.com

If you have to use plastic for purchases, visit Cardweb first.

250 Bankrate

http://www.bankrate.com

At this site there is a huge amount of personal financial information—mortgage, equity loan, credit card, rates of all kinds, and a lot more.

251 Find the Best Rates

http://www.rate.net
http://www.bestrate.com
http://www.money.com/money/rates

Search these sites for rates, fees, and services for many financial products—credit cards, savings accounts, certificates of deposit, and loans.

252 Dollar Stretcher

http://www.stretcher.com

This site's motto is "live better for less." Just about anything you can spend a buck on is discussed here.

253 Book It

http://www.quicken.com

Quicken takes care of your bookkeeping and will help keep you fiscally sound on the Net. It has several major categories that include investing, mortgage, insurance, taxes, banking, and retirement.

254 Cost of Living

http://www.jsc.nasa.gov/bu2/inflate.html
http://woodrow.mpls.frb.fed.us/economy/calc/cpihome.html
http://www.NewsEngin.com/neFreeTools.nsf/CPIcalc

What is a dollar worth? After visiting these sites, you'll know.

255 Salary Calculation

http://www.paycheckcity.com
http://www.homefair.com/homefair/cmr/salcalc.html

Compare your current situation with some other scenarios. Cost-of-living factors and other issues are also covered at these sites.

256 What Am I Worth?

http://salarycenter.monster.com
http://www.acinet.org

At these sites, you'll find out and will also get a lot of tips about salary issues.

257   He Gets Paid What?

http://www.paywatch.org
http://www.wageweb.com

Compare your salary to compensation packages of some of the
big boys. For example, it might take you five hundred years to
earn what these CEOs made last year. Then learn at Wageweb
what we regular folks earn.

258   Tax Planet

http://www.taxplanet.com

If you live on this planet, you pay taxes. Gary Klott, a syndicated
columnist, has a great year-round guide to understanding taxes.

259   Tax Time

http://www.irs.gov
http://www.taxsites.com

During these taxing times, you might want to read the tax code (all
six thousand pages of it). Happy filing.

260   The Tax Foundation

http://www.taxfoundation.org

Learn a lot about your tax dollars. For example, the average
American has to work until May each year just to pay his tax bill for
that year.

261   Death and . . .

http://www.taxprophet.com
http://www.tax.org/Quotes/quotations.htm

. . . taxes. These sites provide advice and some funny quotes
about taxes. What could possibly be funny about taxes?

Social Security Administration

http://www.ssa.gov

The SSA has a very pretty page. You can request your Social Security benefit statement at this site. Go for it.

401(k)

http://www.401kafe.com

We hear about 401(k)s all the time. Let this café provide you with tips, calculators, learning tools, and other timely information about these important retirement accounts.

Wills and Trusts

http://www.mtpalermo.com

This is a free crash course in wills and trusts put together by Michael Palermo, attorney and certified financial planner.

Estate Planning

http://www.estateplanforyou.com
http://www.estateattorney.com
http://www.freeadvice.com
http://www.nolo.com/encyclopedia/ep_ency.html

Prior, proper planning prevents problems with your estate, and these sites will help.

"I found something really gross and disgusting on
the Internet—my school lunch menu!"

>> *Food, Diet & Nutrition*

 266 **Epicurious**

> http://www.epicurious.com
>
> If it has to do with food and drink, it will be here.

 267 **What's in That Burger?**

> http://www.olen.com/food
>
> Learn the nutritional information of more than one thousand fast-food items.

268 **The Web Gourmet**

> http://www.tubears.com
> http://www.gourmetspot.com
>
> These gourmets are glad to provide you with fifty thousand recipes and other treats.

 269 **Everything but the Kitchen Sink**

> http://www.kitchenlink.com
> http://www.recipecenter.com
> http://www.foodtv.com
>
> Learn everything about food, cooking, recipes, and the kitchen.

270 ## Food on the Web

http://www.foodweb.com

http://www.restaurantreport.com/Top100

These sites concentrate on food, dining, and the good life.

271 ## Secret Recipes

http://www.topsecretrecipes.com

Want to know how to make those delicious Doubletree Hotel chocolate chip cookies? Visit this site for that and many other secret recipes.

272 ## The Science of Cooking

http://www.inquisitivecook.com

The concept is: If you understand what ingredients do and how they work together, the mystery will be taken out of cooking.

273 ## Cookies Galore

http://www.cookierecipe.com

http://www.cookiegarden.com

There's nothing better than home-baked cookies. Get some recipes here. And if you can't bake, just order them online.

274 ## It's Candy Time

http://www.candyusa.org

At this site, it sure is. Just don't tell your dentist.

275 ## Menus and Food Reviews

http://www.zagat.com

http://www.restaurantrow.com

If you are hungry, check out a menu. Of course, see Zagat's restaurant reviews first.

276 Rating Restaurants

http://www.dinesite.com

Find restaurants that are rated using different criteria. If you've been to one of these establishments, rate it!

277 Big Tipper

http://www.tipping.org

Become an educated tipper. Here's to great service.

278 Do You Wine?

http://wine.wsj.com
http://www.wines.com
http://www.winespectator.com
http://www.wineloverspage.com

Learn to be a connoisseur at these sites.

279 Shake It Up, Baby

http://www.webtender.com
http://www.idrink.com

Let's make a toast. If you want to know anything about mixed drinks, these are your sites.

280 Calorie Conscious

http://www.caloriecontrol.org
http://www.dietitian.com

Fat is the great American obsession. These two sites will help keep you fit and trim.

281 Favorite Conversation

http://www.diettalk.com

Diettalk is a directory of good diet information. Start with the calculator section, and proceed from there.

282 Watch Your Weight

http://www.dietwatch.com

Here's an Internet support group for watching your weight. Come for a visit and a tour.

283 What's Your Goal?

http://www.ediets.com
http://www.dietsite.com

This site will help you choose healthy foods when dining, get diet advice, and obtain up-to-date and straightforward nutrition information.

284 Nutrition Navigator

http://navigator.tufts.edu

Tufts University rates nutrition sites on the Net. This site gets an A+.

285 Focus on Nutrition

http://www.nutritionnewsfocus.com

Take charge of your own nutrition. Review articles, ask experts, and receive a daily e-mail newsletter.

>> Free Stuff

 ### I Wanna Be Free

http://www.4freestuff.com
http://freebies.about.com
http://www.freeshop.com
http://www.freemania.net

Who said nothing is free? Visit these sites to see all that is available.

 ### Get it for Free

http://www.free.com
http://www.weeklyfreebie.com
http://www.100percentfreestuff.com

There are many free things on the Net; these sites lead you in the right direction.

 ### Kid Freebies

http://www.webfreebees.net/kidslinks

Here is a lot of fun and free stuff for the little ones.

"My dad is afraid I'm turning into a computer weenie, so I told him I joined the trackball team."

>> *Games*

 289 ### Are You a Millionaire?

http://www.lottonet.com
http://www.lottobot.net

What are the winning lottery numbers? If you do win, please remember me!

290 ### Game Time

http://www.station.sony.com
http://www.gamespot.com
http://www.boxerjam.com

Have fun playing games at these sites, including Jeopardy, Wheel of Fortune, and other classics.

291 ### Classic Cards

http://hoyle.won.net

Play card games, board games, and much more at Hoyle's site.

292 ### Games Galore

http://games.go.com
http://games.yahoo.com

Head on over to these professional game portal sites for hours of fun.

293 ### Come Play with Me

http://www.playsite.com

Play chess, checkers, or backgammon with other connected people. In the future, this will probably become a way of life. Check it out today.

294 ### It's Game Time

http://www.happypuppy.com

This site has nothing to do with dogs. It is known as one of the better sites for games. Have some fun.

295 ### Games Mania

http://www.gamesmania.com

The title says it all. Want to have some fun with games? Check it out.

296 ### Games for Dummies

http://www.gamepro.com

Here is a very nice game site from the folks who brought you the *Dummies* books.

297 ### Game Time Help

http://sages.ign.com
http://www.thecheatersguild.com

Are you having trouble with one of your games? Let these sites assist you with winning.

298 ### Headbone

http://www.headbone.com

Play games, chat, and other stuff at Headbone.

299 Bonus.com

http://www.bonus.com

This is a super site for fun. If you're a kid, go to this playground.

300 Fun Brain!

http://www.funbrain.com

Have fun while learning—what a novel idea! Play these games and learn a lot.

301 Funology

http://www.funology.com

Have some fun. This site will teach you a million and one ways to make things, explore the world, and discover skills you never knew you had. This is one place where you'll never be bored.

302 Solve-it Mysteries

http://www.mysterynet.com

Use the Web, learn, and have fun while you challenge your critical thinking skills. Unravel case mysteries at "Solve-it."

303 Arcade City

http://www.freearcade.com

Kill some time by playing games at this free arcade.

304 Playtime

http://www.zone.com

From action to strategy, you should have lots of fun playing these games. Thousands of people are online at one time enjoying the games.

305   ## DuJour

http://www.dujour.com

Here's a fun-filled path to Internet Nirvana. You'll find games and contests guaranteed to titillate, challenge, and annoy.

306   ## "Let There Be Fun"

http://www.uproar.com

That's the motto here. There are many quizzes to take, so pick a category and let the fun begin!

307   ## The Puzzle Depot

http://www.puzzledepot.com
http://www.puzzlecenter.com

You'll find crosswords, riddles and word puzzles, logic and strategy board game software, and a large selection of shareware.

308   ## Think Puzzles

http://www.dailypuzzler.com
http://www.thinks.com

These sites are where to go for your daily fix of crossword puzzles, word games, logic games, jumbles, word searches, and trivia.

309   ## Crossword Puzzles

http://www.dailycrossword.com
http://www.crosswordweaver.com
http://www.oneacross.com
http://www.ojohaven.com/fun/crossword.html

Get your keyboard ready and prepare to solve these puzzles. If you need some help with a word, try the last two sites.

310 **Putting the Pieces Together**

http://www.jigzone.com

Jigsaw puzzle fans will love this site. Choose from hundreds of puzzles of all degrees of difficulty. Move the pieces with your mouse, time yourself and—if you get stuck—tell it to solve itself.

311 **Quiz Me**

http://www.quizsite.com

Discover lots of fun quizzes here. You can select subject area and level of difficulty.

312 **Quizzes Are Fun**

http://www.coolquiz.com

All kinds of quizzes for music, quotes, TV, movies, and more can be found at this very cool site.

313 **Meet the Wizard**

http://www.thewizardofodds.com

I bet you will be a much better gambler after visiting this site.

314 **Pinball Wizard**

http://www.pinball.net
http://www.lysator.liu.se/pinball

Who would have thought—a comprehensive Web site about pinball?

>> *Geography*

315 My Country 'Tis of Thee

http://www.your-nation.com

Which country's population has the longest life expectancy? You'll find the answer to this question and many more at this site.

316 National Geographic

http://www.nationalgeographic.com

The famed organization is now online. If you enjoy its detailed reporting on nature, science, and the world around us, do not miss this site.

317 Geo Globe

http://library.advanced.org/10157

Play a geography game at this site. You choose the level from beginner to advanced.

318 Library of Congress Studies Countries

http://lcweb2.loc.gov/frd/cs/cshome.html

Get detailed information on most countries here.

319 Can We All Get Along?

http://www.iearn.org

The International Education and Resource Network enables young people to tackle projects designed to make a meaningful contribution to the health and welfare of the planet and its people.

320 3D Atlas

http://www.nationalatlas.gov

Here's great stuff about geography, and the maps are in 3D. Cool!

321 Demographics Galore

http://www.easidemographics.com

If you need a little or a lot of information about a specific geographic area, you can get it here.

322 This Is Geography

http://members.aol.com/bowermanb/101.html

Take a tour of the world of geography with Mr. Bowerman. This is a very nice resource for many geographic details.

323 Country Information

http://www.excite.com/travel/countries

If you need information on any country, state, or city, check out Excite's detailed resources.

324 Countries Online

http://www.atlapedia.com
http://www.geographic.org

These sites contain some key information about every country of the world—facts and details about geography, climate, people, religion, language, history, and economy.

325 Get Help from the CIA

http://www.odci.gov/cia/publications/factbook/index.html

If you're doing a project about any country, the CIA would like to assist you.

326 **States Online**

http://www.piperinfo.com/state/states.html
http://govinfo.kerr.orst.edu

Get a lot of information about states here.

327 **Capitals**

http://www.50states.com
http://www.capitals.com

Here you can match a capital with the state, hear the state song, and see trivia and many facts about U.S. states and most countries.

328 **The United Nations**

http://www.un.org
http://www.unep.net
http://www.unol.org
http://www.unsystem.org

Every school kid can now say, "I have been to the United Nations."

329 **Ain't No Mountain High Enough**

http://www.americasroof.com

Find out the tallest elevation in each state and around the world.

330 **Vexillology**

http://www.flags.net
http://fotw.digibel.be/flags

These sites are dedicated to the study of flags.

>> *Government*

331 **The National Debt**

http://www.brillig.com/debt_clock

How much is the U.S. debt? Check the clock for details of this staggering sum.

332 **True or False?**

http://cagle.slate.msn.com/art/3GovtTRUE.asp

These are actual facts about the U.S. government, and Daryl Cagle has an unusual way of presenting the information.

333 **NARA**

http://www.nara.gov

The National Archives and Records Administration is the government agency that is responsible for overseeing the management of federal government records. Be sure to check out the Exhibit Hall and Internet resources.

334 **Census Data**

http://factfinder.census.gov
http://icg.fas.harvard.edu/~census

Simply and easily, get census data about any area in the U.S.

335 **The Branches . . .**

http://www.supremecourtus.gov
http://thomas.loc.gov
http://bioguide.congress.gov
http://www.whitehouse.gov

. . . of U.S. government.

Citizen's Government Guide

http://www.erols.com/irasterb/gov.htm

Poppa Sterby has created the ultimate site about the U.S. government. Check out his fine work.

 ### All the Presidents

http://www.americanpresidents.org

C-SPAN knows presidents, and they're all here for your reading and listening pleasure.

 ### The CIA Knows Kids

http://www.odci.gov/cia/ciakids/index.html

It should be enough that your parents are keeping an eye on you. Maybe the CIA is also watching.

 ### Government Portal

http://www.firstgov.gov

You can easily search U.S. government information that has been posted on the Internet. This site offers an index to help you find what you need.

 ### Federal Statistics

http://www.fedstats.gov

More than seventy agencies in the United States federal government produce statistics of interest to the public. You'll find them here.

341 Uncle Sam

http://www.uncle-sam.com

http://www.capweb.net

http://www.govspot.com

These sites provide a citizen's guide to the U.S. government on the World Wide Web.

342 Home of the Brave

http://www.military.com

http://www.searchmil.com

Here are sites for those men and women who have served in the military.

343 Portal to War

http://www.wtj.com/portal

This is a good resource for researchers, hobbyists, military professionals, and others with an interest in military history, science, and defense.

344 Take Me to Your Leader

http://www.trytel.com/~aberdeen

http://www.geocities.com/Athens/1058/rulers.html

Who runs the countries of the world? Find out here. You can also obtain their mailing addresses and Web sites.

345 Inaugural Speeches and More

http://www.bartleby.com/124/index.html

http://www.pbs.org/greatspeeches

From George Washington to the current president, they're all represented here.

346 Mr. President

http://www.ibiblio.org/lia/president
http://www.grolier.com/presidents/preshome.html
http://www.pbs.org/presidents

Every U.S. president is listed at these sites.

347 What's Your Policy?

http://www.policy.com
http://www.intellectualcapital.com
http://www.speakout.com

Policies and the issues of the day can be found and debated at these rather stimulating sites.

348 The Royal Family

http://www.royal.gov.uk
http://www.princeofwales.gov.uk

The British Royal family has gone online.

>> Grammar & Words

349 BTW

http://www.acronymfinder.com

Acronyms got you baffled? YNA (You're not alone). Here's a searchable database containing common acronyms and abbreviations about all subjects, with a special focus on computers, technology, telecommunications, and the military.

350 Fun with Words

http://www.fun-with-words.com

http://www.wolinskyweb.com/word.htm

Anagrams, palindromes, and many interesting word games are available at this fun site.

351 Vocabulary Builder

http://www.wordsmith.org/awad/index.html

Want to sound smart? Use the words that this wordsmith will e-mail to you each and every day.

352 Vocabulary University

http://www.vocabulary.com

Participate in these vocabulary puzzles to promote word mastery.

353 Big Words in the News

http://www.mcs.net/~kvj/spizz.html

How's your vocabulary? Look at a list of unusual words that have appeared in recent news articles, and try to guess the definitions.

354 The Word Detective

http://www.word-detective.com

Did you ever wonder where phrases like "lame duck" came from? Visit The Word Detective for the answer.

Irregardless

http://www.mavensword.com

Is it a word? Well, check out the Mavens' Word of the Day and find out about a lot of words.

 ### English 101

http://www.bartleby.com/141/index.html
http://www.wsu.edu:8080/~brians/errors/errors.html

These sites will keep your grammar in check.

 ### Grammar and Style

http://www.grammarnow.com
http://www.grammarlady.com
http://andromeda.rutgers.edu/~jlynch/Writing

Most of us can use some assistance with our use of the English language. Ain't that the truth!

>> Greeting Cards

Greetings Everyone

http://www.100topcardsites.com
http://www.bluemountain.com
http://www.ohmygoodness.com
http://greetings.yahoo.com

There are many greeting sites on the Net; these will get you started. Go ahead and send a friend or a loved one a virtual greeting.

359 ## Greetings

http://www.greetst.com

http://www.hallmark.com

http://www.cardmaster.com

E-mail cards are very popular on the Net. Here are some great sites for sending greeting cards.

360 ## Send a Postcard

http://www.mypostcards.net

http://www.postcards.org

Send a postcard for almost any occasion, or even just for a practical joke.

361 ## Greetings with Music

http://greetings.mp3.com

MP3 is a hot technology on the Net. Now you can send a card along with music.

362 ## Virtual Flowers

http://www.virtualflowers.com

http://www.800florals.com/virtual

http://www.flowernetwork.com/virtual-b

For Valentines Day, a birthday, or maybe just a fun way to say, "I'm thinking of you," send one of your friends some flowers.

"You've been working too hard. Instead of a
heartbeat, I'm getting a fax tone."

>> Health & Medicine

363 ### Health on the Net

http://www.hon.ch
http://www.hiethics.org

When you visit health sites on the Net, you may sometimes see the
HON logo. To earn this logo, the site must subscribe to all eight of
the principles of credibility that HON developed.

364 ### Empowerment for All

http://www.wemedia.com

This site's stated mission is "to empower persons with disabilities,
their families, and friends by being a conduit for education,
knowledge, technology, entertainment, and numerous other
services in an exciting, convenient, and accessible fashion."

365 ### Medical Terminology

http://www.medterms.com
http://www3.bc.sympatico.ca/me/patientsguide/medterms.htm
http://www3.bc.sympatico.ca/me/patientsguide/glossary.htm

Medical terms can be a little bewildering. Here are some online
medical term dictionaries.

366 The Merck Manual

http://merckhomeedition.com

The world famous Merck Manual is at this site. You'll also find quizzes and other interesting facts.

367 Physician's Desk Reference

http://consumer.pdr.net/consumer

This trusted name has a Getting Well Network and many other news and information sources.

368 You First

http://www.youfirst.com

Taking control of your health begins with a better understanding of factors discussed here.

369 Family Health Radio

http://www.fhradio.org

Hosted by Ohio University, this site contains some practical, easy-to-understand answers to some of the most frequently asked questions about health and health care. You'll also find a series of articles dating back to 1993.

370 I'll Never Grow Up

http://future.newsday.com/2/quiz.htm

The Internet knows all. Go to this site, answer the questions, and quickly find out your life expectancy.

371 My Real Age

http://www.realage.com

Answer a few questions, and this site will let you know how old you really are.

AMA on the Net

http://www.ama-assn.org

The American Medical Association has a site on the Net. If you want to search for a doctor, there are over 650,000 MDs listed.

 ## Kids Health

http://www.ama-assn.org/ama/pub/category/1947.html
http://www.healthfinder.gov/kids

The American Medical Association and the U.S. Department of Health and Human Services provide a wealth of information about children's health. Go for a checkup.

 ## Direct Me to Health

http://www.hospitalselect.com
http://www.hospitaldirectory.com

This site is more than just a hospital directory. Try out the life expectancy questionnaire or the health news directory for complete reporting on most health care topics.

 ## Doctors On Call

http://www.americasdoctor.com

Here are real doctors, real answers, real time—twenty-four hours a day. Chat with a doctor, join a community, or read timely articles.

 ## Board Certified

http://www.abms.org

It seems that many people are afraid to ask their doctors if they are board certified. Well, don't ask. Just go to this site to find out.

377 What's Up Doc?

http://www.docguide.com

This doc will guide you to information and sites that are intended to assist doctors and patients.

378 Dr. Quackwatch

http://www.quackwatch.com

Dr. Stephen Barrett calls this site "Your Guide to Health Fraud, Quackery, and Intelligent Decisions."

379 Ask the Doctor

http://www.drweil.com
http://www.drkoop.com

On and off the Net, these doctors have assisted many folks.

380 Virtual Medical Center

http://www.medscape.com

Need some medical information? Check out this excellent search engine and information source.

381 Get Healthy!

http://www.healthfinder.gov
http://www.healthatoz.com

These sites will assist you in living a healthy lifestyle. Don't forget to occasionally turn off the Net, go outside, get some exercise, and breathe the fresh air.

Your Health . . .

http://www.yourhealth.com

http://www.yourhealth.com/ahl

. . . is very important. Every weeknight you can chat with a different health expert. You'll also find an audio health library where hundreds of topics are addressed in detail.

Health Online

http://www.stayhealthy.com

http://www.personalmd.com

http://www3.bc.sympatico.ca/me/patientsguide

Your health is your most valuable asset. Use these sites to assist in maintaining a healthy lifestyle.

Health Care

http://www.achoo.com

http://www.healthanswers.com

http://www.allhealth.com

http://www.healthyideas.com

You can never be too healthy. Here are some sites that will help ensure your health.

Thrive Online

http://www.thriveonline.com

Whether we're online or offline, we should all be able to stay a bit healthier with help from this site.

386 Online Pharmacy

http://www.merckmedco.com
http://www.drugstore.com
http://www.cvs.com
http://www.walgreens.com

From providing a complete drug index to taking your order for various medications, these sites are your prescriptions for great information.

387 Medication Bible

http://www.rxlist.com
http://www.drugdigest.org
http://www.drugchecker.com

Learn about medications, drug interactions, and more at these drug sites.

388 Clinical Trials

http://www.centerwatch.com
http://www.acurian.com
http://www.hopelink.com
http://www.veritasmedicine.com

Clinical trials, studies, research, and new therapies can be found here.

389 Feelin' All Right

http://www.aromaweb.com
http://www.aromaessentials.com

Aromatherapy is defined as the use of volatile plant oils—including essential oils—to help achieve psychological and physical well-being.

390 **American Council for Drug Education**

http://www.acde.org

Get educated about this difficult problem area.

391 **Smoke-Free Kids**

http://www.tobaccofreekids.org

Here are a couple of scary stats from this site: "Three thousand children start smoking every day; one third will eventually die from their addiction."

392 **Smoke-Free**

http://quitsmoking.about.com
http://www.quitsmokingsupport.com

If you're a smoker and want to quit, check out these sites that will help you kick the habit.

>> History

393 **History Net**

http://www.thehistorynet.com

When it comes to history, this site has it all.

394 **The History Channel**

http://www.historychannel.com
http://www.historyplace.com

The past comes alive—online.

395 History at a Glance

http://www.hyperhistory.com

This is an interesting way to present the history of the world.

396 History Professor

http://www.historesearch.com
http://www.ukans.edu/history/VL

Professor Jenkins and the history department (Univ. of Kansas) did their homework. You'll find information about U.S. history, world history, and more.

397 An Abridged History of the United States

http://www.us-history.com

This author wants all students to develop a basic understanding of our history.

398 U.S. Civil War

http://www.uscivilwar.com
http://www.civilwar.com

Get details about the war, and find links that will take you to other sites.

399 Early America

http://www.earlyamerica.com

At this site you'll find a magazine, pictures, certain historical documents, and more.

400 History 102

http://us.history.wisc.edu/hist102

Get a good dose of American history from the Civil War to the present.

401 In 1492, Columbus Sailed the Ocean Blue

http://lcweb.loc.gov/exhibits/1492/intro.html

Columbus may be less politically correct today, but here is a site that has a lot of information about him and his travels.

402 How the West Was Found

http://www.pbs.org/lewisandclark

Travel back in time with Lewis and Clark.

403 World Heritage

http://www.unesco.org/whc/heritage.htm

The Galapagos, the Grand Canyon, and over five hundred other sites are here. These cultural and natural sites constitute a common heritage, to be treasured as unique testimonies to an enduring past.

404 Egyptology

http://www.kv5.com
http://library.thinkquest.org/15924

Go to these sites to live, learn, and even feel the excitement of ancient Egypt.

405 **World Wars**

http://www.worldwar1.com
http://4worldwarII.4anything.com
http://www.wtj.com/portal

Were these the wars to end all wars? Not exactly, but here are sites to educate you about WWI and WWII.

406 **Let's Talk History**

http://www.talkinghistory.org
http://www.hpol.org

These folks provide a comprehensive collection of audio documentaries, speeches, debates, a few oral histories, commentaries, and more. Listen to these extraordinary sites.

407 **Famous Speeches**

http://gos.sbc.edu
http://douglass.speech.nwu.edu

Thank you, Sweet Briar College and Northwestern University for archiving these famous speeches.

408 **Living in the Past**

http://www.adflip.com
http://www.retroactive.com
http://www.fiftythings.com
http://www.hometownfavorites.com

Ah, the good old days. If you want to go back a few years, these sites will show you some great stuff.

>> *Holidays*

409 ### Holiday Celebrations

http://www.holidays.net

Who doesn't love holidays? Happy celebrating.

410 ### Holidays around the World

http://www.holidayfestival.com

This site will allow you to determine the holidays in any country.

411 ### Every Day's a Holiday

http://www.earthcalendar.net
http://www.theholidayspot.com

Pick any day on the calendar and find out which holidays are being celebrated.

412 ### Haunted America

http://www.halloweenguide.com

It has become a huge celebration. Join the fun and horror at this online guide to Halloween.

413 ### Happy Thanksgiving

http://www.night.net/thanksgiving
http://www.butterball.com

You can have an Internet Thanksgiving with (almost) all the trimmings.

414 **What's Up, Santa?**

http://www.northpole.com
http://www.claus.com

Any time of the year you can have some fun at the North Pole.

>> Home & Real Estate

415 **Improvement on the Net**

http://www.improvenet.com

Got a home-improvement project in mind? This site will help with ideas and even find a prescreened contractor to assist with the project.

416 **Let's Get Handy**

http://www.nari.org
http://www.naturalhandyman.com

These sites are for the home-improvement person. You can even ask questions. So, Bob Vila and Tim Allen, the Net is catching up to you.

417 **Home 101**

http://www.ahahome.com
http://www.housenet.com
http://www.homearts.com
http://www.hgtv.com

Everything you ever needed to know about home ownership and maintenance can be found here.

418 Home Life

http://www.livinghome.com

If you have a house, you will need all the resources this site has—home calculators, gardening tips, and a host of other things.

419 Ask the Builder

http://www.askbuild.com

Tim Carter has an excellent site. You can ask him any question about your home and read the articles that he writes about home projects.

420 This Old House

http://www.bobvila.com
http://www.hometime.com

Do you love watching home-improvement shows on TV? Well, now you can catch them on the Net!

421 It's a Good Thing

http://www.marthastewart.com

Online, you can enjoy Martha Stewart twenty-four hours a day.

422 Green Thumb

http://www.gardenweb.com
http://www.garden.com
http://www.gardenguides.com
http://www.gardenreview.com

Everything you ever wanted to know about your garden is all on the Web.

423 Ask a Question

http://www.yardcare.com

http://www.bhglive.com/gardening/db/findhome.htm

These sites will allow you to ask questions and search for your garden needs.

424 Use It

http://www.wackyuses.com

Learn how to use everyday products in unusual, helpful ways. To clean a toilet, for example, drop in two Alka-Seltzer tablets, wait twenty minutes, brush, and flush.

425 Real Estate on the Net

http://www.realtor.com

http://www.domania.com

Search among a million home listings, and find the selling prices of millions of others.

426 Real Estate Searching

http://www.realestate.com

http://realestate.yahoo.com

http://homeadvisor.msn.com

http://www.lycos.com/realestate

Many of the search engines have gone into the real estate business. Search for your dream home here.

427 Mortgage.com

http://www.iown.com

Everything from mortgage rates to the resale price of comparable homes in your neighborhood, you'll find it all at this site.

Mortgage Net

> http://www.mortgage-net.com
> http://mortgage.quicken.com
>
> Here are the ultimate mortgage sites. There are historical and current rates and tons of other stuff. If you're in the home market, camp out here for a while.

 Premier Source for Mortgage Info!

> http://www.hsh.com
> http://www.homeowners.com
> http://www.mortgage101.com
>
> These are some excellent sites for home mortgage information, calculators, and much more.

 Mortgage Prepayment Calculator

> http://www.bloomberg.com/cgi-bin/ilpc.cgi
>
> Compliments of *Bloomberg*, this is an easy-to-use mortgage calculator. You can also identify how prepayment will affect your mortgage payoff.

 Mortgage, Finance Calculators, and More

> http://www.interest.com/hugh/calc
> http://www.wolinskyweb.com/measure.htm
>
> If a calculator is on the Net, you'll find it here.

 On the Move

> http://www.relocationcentral.com
> http://www.monstermoving.com
>
> If you are moving somewhere or just want to know about another city (worldwide coverage), check out these sites. There are also such interesting features as a salary calculator.

433 **Buy Furniture Online?**

http://www.furniturefind.com
http://www.furniturefan.com

Sit down, relax, and enjoy researching and actually purchasing your furniture via the Net.

>> Homework & Study Aids

434 **Homework Heaven?**

http://www.homeworkheaven.com

Give this site to your kids, and tell them to stop their complaining.

435 **Homework Helper**

http://www.schoolwork.org

Library closed? Need some information for your homework assignments? Schoolwork Ugh! might be your solution.

436 **Homework Hits the Spot**

http://www.homeworkspot.com

StartSpot Mediaworks is well-known for creating amazing Web sites. This one is dedicated to providing sites and information to assist with homework.

437 **Links for Learning**

http://www.studyweb.com

With over one hundred forty thousand educational links, you'll be chained to the Net for a while.

438 **Note It**

http://www.sparknotes.com

http://www.gradesaver.com

About one hundred Harvard students have contributed notes and information on subjects ranging from astronomy to psychology.

439 **Novel Idea**

http://www.novelguide.com

Here's a guide for better understanding of classic and contemporary literature through chapter summaries, character profiles, metaphor analysis, theme analyses, and author biographies.

440 **Smart Monkey**

http://www.pinkmonkey.com

This monkey has a comprehensive digital library, literature notes, and study guides focused on core academic subjects, test preparation materials, and links to other educational sites.

441 **B.J. Pinchbeck's Homework Helper**

http://www.bjpinchbeck.com

B.J. says, "If you can't find it here, then you just can't find it!" He has one heck of a site. By the way, he is thirteen years old.

442 **The Internet Schoolhouse**

http://www.internetschoolhouse.com

This is an excellent site that has information on just about any subject. Check it out; you'll be glad you attended.

443 **Research Papers**

http://www.researchpaper.com

We all have to do them, and this is the place to get some help.

444 Cliffs Notes

http://www.cliffs.com

You know them well, and this is a well-designed site. There is some great information, and it's a fun site to visit.

>> *Insurance*

445 Life and Health Insurance

http://www.life-line.org

Here is straightforward and unbiased information on insurance—life and health.

446 Insurance Ratings

http://www.ambest.com/ratings/search.html
http://www.insureclick.com

Purchasing insurance can be confusing. These sites should insure that you get the best product for your needs.

447 Quote Me on This

http://www.quickquote.com
http://www.insweb.com

Use these sites for quotes on insurance, moving, realtors, and more.

448 Insurance Guide

http://www.insure.com
http://insurance.yahoo.com

The Yahoo! site is a comprehensive insurance center, and insure.com says, "We inform, you decide."

"Hello, technical support?"

>> Internet

 Web Novice

http://www.folksonline.com
http://www.livinginternet.com

There are many people who are new to the Net. Check out these sites for help.

 I'm a Newbie

http://www.getnetwise.org
http://www.ozline.com/learning/webtypes.html

Kids and educators will enjoy using these sites to learn the ins and outs of the Net.

 Test Your Knowledge

http://www.netsurfquiz.com

Have some fun and take these Internet quizzes; each week you'll find a new one. There's lots of other trivia and fun here, too.

 Bust 'Em

http://www.scambusters.org

Learn about Internet scams and become a more informed Web surfer.

453 **History of the Net**

http://www.isoc.org/internet-history
http://www.theatlantic.com/unbound/flashbks/computer/bushf.htm

Learn all the details about the origins and evolution of the Internet.

454 **World Domains**

http://www.theodora.com/country_digraphs.html

We all know about .com, but did you know that every country in the world has its own unique domain suffix? Visit this site to connect all the dots to their respective countries.

455 **Portal about Portals**

http://www.traffick.com

Web sites that provide all of your information in one place have become popular. Now there is a site that reports on these portals.

456 **Internet News**

http://www.newslinx.com
http://www.internetnews.com

These sites are excellent for obtaining technology news stories from some of the major publications on the Net. They allow you to scan titles and decide if you want to read the stories.

457 **Net.com**

http://www.internet.com
http://www.webopedia.com

Keep informed about Internet news. From stocks to resources, you'll find it here.

458 Internet News and Law

http://www.cnet.com
http://www.zdnet.com
http://www.news.com
http://www.gigalaw.com

When it comes to Internet news and law, these are some of the best resources.

459 Free Internet Access

http://www.freedomlist.com
http://www.hereontheweb.com/freeinternet.htm

It almost sounds too good to be true. These sites rate many of the free Internet service providers.

460 Speed It Up

http://www.speed411.com
http://msn.zdnet.com/partners/msn/bandwidth/speedtest500.htm

How fast is your Internet connection? Go to this site and you'll know in a flash.

461 Protect Thy PC

http://www.zonealarm.com

If your computer is continuously online, you should protect yourself from Internet thieves, vandals, and hackers. This highly-rated product should help.

462 Internet in the Sky

http://www.teledesic.com

It's a bird, it's a plane . . . no, it's Internet access brought to you via satellite.

463 **The I Way**

http://www.idrive.com

http://www.xdrive.com

Computer data backups are important. How would you like to store some of your files on the Net? It's a great way to have off-site backups and access to your files from any Internet connection.

464 **Remind Me**

http://www.netmind.com

If you want to be reminded when a certain Web site is updated, this site will keep you informed.

465 **Stroud's Internet Software Resource**

http://cws.internet.com

This site can be your one-stop shopping location for the latest and greatest Internet software.

466 **Virus Myths**

http://www.vmyths.com

Tired of getting those chain e-mail messages about viruses? This site lets you know if a virus is real or a myth. Here's to your computer's good health.

>> Inventions & Patents

467 **Inventor's Hall of Fame**

http://www.invent.org/book/index.html

And you thought the Hall of Fame was only for sports heroes. Check out these clever folks who have invented a lot of incredible stuff.

Patents Galore

http://www.delphion.com

http://www.patentmodel.org

The Intellectual Property Network lets you access over twenty-six years of U.S. Patent and Trademark Office patent descriptions as well as the last ten years of images. The first entries date back to January 5, 1971. You can search, retrieve, and study over two million patents.

 Quest for Patent Validity

http://www.bountyquest.com

BountyQuest is on a mission to strengthen the patent system. It will pay cash rewards to people who can help find evidence critical to issues of patent validity.

>> *Kids Sites*

 Yahoo! for Kids

http://www.yahooligans.com

When it comes to knowing where to find things on the Net, Yahoo! is one of the leaders. See what sites it recommends for you.

471　It's All about Kids

http://kidsinternet.about.com
http://kidexchange.about.com
http://www.cyberkids.com

The Internet is a great playground and educational tool for kids. These sites will lead you to many fine resources on the Net.

472　We're All Kids

http://www.kidscom.com

You might think this site is just for younger kids, but it's for the kid in all of us. Find out all about holidays, the heart, and tons of other stuff here.

473　Kids Linking around the World

http://www.kidlink.org

This organization joins kids from the ages of ten to fifteen together for a global dialogue.

474　Kid's Bank

http://www.kidsbank.com

Here are interesting money facts and calculators. Adults might even learn a thing or two.

475　Young Bucks

http://www.younginvestor.com
http://www.kidstock.com

Explore monetary issues for teenagers. Learn about financial matters while you're young.

Make *TIME* for Kids

http://www.sikids.com

http://www.timeforkids.com

On the Net, Time Warner has great content for kids. You'll find *Sports Illustrated* and *TIME* magazine have interesting and timely information.

 Children's Express

http://www.cenews.org

At this site, you will find information and news for kids. Serious and fun things are there for you.

>> Language

 Language Translation

http://www.freetranslation.com

http://translator.go.com

http://babelfish.altavista.com

You can translate a word, phrase, or even an entire Web page here.

 Translating Dictionaries

http://www.logos.it

http://dictionaries.travlang.com

Have a word translated into many languages.

Languages of the World

http://www.june29.com/HLP

http://www.sil.org/ethnologue

These sites provide a comprehensive catalog of language-related resources.

"Don't just sit there, son—surf the Net!"

>> Learning

481 **The Discovery Channel**

http://www.discovery.com
http://school.discovery.com

Discovery has always made learning interesting, and it is no different on the Net. There is even a special kids' section.

482 **The Knowledge Portal**

http://www.hungrymindsuniversity.com

The more I know, the more I know that I don't know. Get educated by signing up for some courses on the Net.

483 **Personal Trainer**

http://www.myprimetime.com

This is your "training" site for the subjects of home, money, work, health, and play.

484 **Smart Alec**

http://www.mensa.org/workout.html

Think you're pretty smart? Head on over to the Mensa Web site and take the test. Good luck.

485 Be Creative

http://www.bemorecreative.com

Spend a couple of hours here and you might learn how to become more creative.

486 Learn Two

http://www.learn2.com
http://www.learn.com

Visit fascinating places where you can learn to do almost anything.

487 Learn How

http://www.ehow.com

From autos to travel, you'll learn how to do almost everything.

488 How Things Work

http://www.howstuffworks.com
http://howthingswork.virginia.edu

Did you ever wonder how some of the things we take for granted work? Well, wonder no more.

489 The Gifted Child

http://www.gifted-children.com

Have an especially bright child? Check out this site for gifted kids and parents.

490 Educational Products

http://www.smarterkids.com

If you need a site to research or buy an educational product, this is it.

>> *Legal*

491 Lawyers, Lawyers, Lawyers

http://www.lawyers.com
http://www.martindale.com
http://www.lawoffice.com

Every lawyer in the land is listed here.

492 Know Nolo

http://www.nolo.com

If it has to do with law, Nolo Press has written about it. From consumer issues to wills, you'll find complete information here—even a few lawyer jokes.

493 Take My Advice

http://www.freeadvice.com

To help people understand their rights, this site provides general information for over a hundred legal topics.

494 Legal Documents

http://www.legaldocs.com
http://www.lawvantage.com
http://www.mylawyer.com
http://www.uscourtforms.com

These creative legal sites offer a preparation service for many types of legal documents.

495 Law Research

http://www.lawresearch.com

Lawyers, this one's for you. Actually, any businessperson should take a look at the many good links at this site.

496 **FindLaw**

http://www.findlaw.com

http://www.catalaw.com

If it has to do with law, no doubt you will find it here, with everything listed by subject from A to W (Anti-Trust to Women).

497 **Emory Law School**

http://www.law.emory.edu/FEDCTS

This site has legal opinions from all of the federal appellate courts and the Supreme Court.

498 **Legal Information Institute**

http://www.law.cornell.edu

Cornell Law School provides an incredible amount of legal resources here.

499 **Law and Order**

http://www.courttv.com

You may not find Perry Mason here, but if you're a courtroom fanatic, you'll love all the information at this site.

500 **Famous Trials**

http://www.law.umkc.edu/faculty/projects/ftrials/ftrials.htm

Most of us are fascinated by important trials, and here are some of the most famous ones.

>> Libraries & Librarians

501 **The Library of Congress**

http://lcweb2.loc.gov

The Library of Congress has an enormous collection, with over sixty exhibits online and many more on the way. The "Today in History" section treats you to a different historical document every day.

502 **American Library Association**

http://www.ala.org
http://www.ala.org/parentspage/greatsites
http://www.ala.org/acrl/resrces.html

The ALA provides leadership for the development, promotion, and improvement of various library and information services, and the profession of librarianship, in order to enhance learning and ensure access to information for all. It also recommends seven hundred great Web sites and other resources.

503 **Library Resource**

http://www.libraryspot.com
http://www.awesomelibrary.org

Libraries and other great resources are available online. These folks have many fine sites for you.

504 **Internet Public Library**

http://www.ipl.org

If you can't find a good piece of information here, you can't find it anywhere.

505 **Librarians**

http://www.lii.org
http://www.clearinghouse.net
http://www.digital-librarian.com

Get to know these hardworking librarians; they have cataloged the Net for you.

>> *Maps*

506 **As the Crow Flies**

http://www.indo.com/cgi-bin/dist

Have some fun calculating distances between places "as the crow flies."

507 **Map That Data**

http://maps.esri.com/esri/mapobjects/tmap/tmap.htm

Now you can take census data and make a colorful map out of it.

508 **Zippy Directions**

http://www.zip2.com

Get the most detailed driving directions on the Net. Also, find out a lot about any city in the U.S.

509 Road Trip!

http://www.freetrip.com
http://www.mapquest.com
http://www.mapsonus.com
http://maps.expedia.com
http://www.earthamaps.com

These sites work a lot like the CD-ROM *Automap*. Just put in your starting point (e.g., Atlanta, GA) and your ending destination (e.g., Charleston, SC), and you will get detailed directions.

510 MapBlaster

http://www.mapblast.com

This unique site allows you to create a map based on a street address that you provide. Another useful feature is that you can then e-mail it to someone. Is a customer coming in from out of town? Let him know where you are located.

511 Maps of the World

http://www.nationalgeographic.com/resources/ngo/maps

This is great for the global village in which we live, especially if you have any need or desire to see a map of anywhere in the world.

512 We're Watching You

http://www.globexplorer.com
http://terraserver.microsoft.com

Don't worry, these are satellite photos. Have some fun and try to find your house.

513 Where in the World?

http://www.astro.ch/atlas

If you need to know where any city in the world is located, this is the place to go.

>> *Math*

514   Simple Calculations

http://www.moneyopolis.org/calc.asp

In life, the simplest things are often the best. Here's a calculator that's easy to use, and you can place it on your toolbar.

515   Add It Up

http://www.calculator.com

You won't believe the variety of online calculators that are available to you at this site.

516   This Does Compute

http://www.wolinskyweb.com/measure.htm
http://www-sci.lib.uci.edu/HSG/RefCalculators.html

Need a calculator? If it isn't at these sites, it just doesn't add up.

517   Conversion Calculators

http://www.megaconverter.com
http://www.microimg.com/science
http://www.cchem.berkeley.edu/ChemResources/temperature.html

U.S. citizens seem to have a problem converting to the metric system and from Fahrenheit to Celsius. Just go to these sites, and these problems will disappear. You'll also find many other conversion calculators as well.

518 **Simple Math**

http://www.NewsEngin.com/neFreeTools.nsf/PercentChange/formPercentChange
http://www.worldwidemetric.com/metcal.htm
http://www.cchem.berkeley.edu/ChemResources/temperature.html

Many of us have trouble dealing with percentage change, the metric system, and making Fahrenheit to Celsius conversions. These sites will keep you cool and calm.

519 **Cornell's Math and Science Gateway**

http://www.tc.cornell.edu/Edu/MathSciGateway

Cornell will provide you with some great resources for the K–12 age group.

520 **Math Resource Center**

http://forum.swarthmore.edu/math.topics.html

This is a great site for the student (K–College) and the teacher.

521 **Flash Cards**

http://www.edu4kids.com/math

Yes, flash cards are on the Net. This site allows you to customize it for the student's level.

522 **Math, Math, and More Math**

http://www.erols.com/bram
http://www.webmath.com

These sites have math for all ages and a number of links to other sites.

Algebra

http://www.algebra-online.com

http://www.quickmath.com

Got an algebra question? This online service can provide the answer.

>> *Movies*

 Movies

http://us.imdb.com

http://movies.yahoo.com

With everything you ever needed to know on the subject, these are the ultimate movie sites.

 A Guide to Movies

http://www.tvguide.com/movies

TV Guide knows movies, and it has information on more than forty thousand films.

 Movie Spot

http://www.cinemaspot.com

This comprehensive movie portal site has reviews, show times, video release dates, award winners, trivia, history, quotes, celebrity gossip, industry resources, and more.

 Movie Buff

http://www.allmovie.com

http://www.movieweb.com

http://www.boxoff.com

http://www.absolutemovies.com

Everything you ever wanted to know about movies can be found at these sites.

528 Hollywood Happenings

http://www.aint-it-cool-news.com

http://www.cinecon.com

What's the movie buzz in Hollywood? These guys have the inside scoop.

529 Movie Mania

http://www.film.com

http://www.littlegoldenguy.com

http://www.oscar.com

Are you a movie fanatic? With these sites, you can have it all. Check out reviews and even two sites dedicated to the little golden guy.

530 Where's It Playing

http://www.moviefone.com

Now that you have decided which movie you want to see, this site will tell you the times and places where it is being shown.

531 My Movie Critic

http://www.moviecritic.com

http://www.cinemascore.com

Give your opinion about some movies, and then let Movie Critic go to work for you. These sites will suggest other movies that you will probably like.

532 Movie Reviews

http://www.mrqe.com

http://www.filmcritic.com

http://www.themovieguys.com

http://www.suntimes.com/ebert/ebertser.html

If you're undecided on what movie to see, let these sites assist.

533 Script-O-Rama

http://www.script-o-rama.com

Drew has over six hundred scripts (movie and television) that you can review.

534 Picky, Picky

http://www.nitpickers.com

Are you the kind of person who likes to find "errors of fact or omission" in movies? Then you'll love this site; there are over eight thousand of them listed here.

535 Bloopers Are Fun

http://www.moviebloopers.com
http://www.movie-mistakes.com

Actors are human. At these sites, learn about many movie bloopers and mistakes.

>> Museums

536 MuseumSpot

http://www.museumspot.com

Enjoy exploring cultural, historical, scientific, and natural attractions from around the world.

537 Cultural Delight

http://www.museumnetwork.com
Discover over 33,000 museums online.

538 Franklin Institute Science Museum

http://www.fi.edu/tfi/welcome.html

This is a museum and a lot more. While you're there, check out the Educational Hotlists.

539 Smithsonian

http://www.si.edu/organiza/start.htm

http://www.si.edu/resource/faq/start.htm

While it is not as rewarding as going in person, these museums are only a click away.

540 Ten Thousand Museums

http://www.elsas.demon.nl/index_e.htm

http://wwar.com/categories/Museums

Use these sites to guide you to more than ten thousand museums all over the world.

541 Museum USA

http://www.museumca.org/usa

The U.S. has a treasure trove of museums, so go for a visit here. There are no lines, and admission is free.

542 Museums and More

http://www.virtualfreesites.com/museums.html

Thousands of museums are just a click away. Take a guided tour.

>> *Music*

543 **MTV and VH1**

http://www.mtv.com
http://www.vh1.com

Cable music channels hit the Net.

544 **MP3**

http://www.mp3.com
http://www.time.com/time/digital/reports/mp3/index.html
http://4mp3audio.4anything.com

Though it actually means "Motion Picture Experts Group Audio
Layer 3," this revolutionary music technology is much more. Learn
all about it, and make your computer into a virtual jukebox.

545 **Musical Extravaganza**

http://mp3.lycos.com
http://www.emusic.com

Use MP3 to download music from the Internet.

546 **Digital Jukebox**

http://www.napster.com
http://www.musicmatch.com

Here's a great match: MUSICMATCH and Napster. Download
music and turn your computer into a digital jukebox.

547 **Music While You Surf**

http://music.lycos.com/radio
http://www.netradio.com

These music stations on the Net offer an incredible selection of
songs, and every kind is covered.

548 WWW on Your Dial

http://www.com

Tune it to this online "radio."

549 Listen Up

http://www.live-online.com

Listen to music on the Net. Live Online is a source for live music cybercasts, chats, and online events.

550 Music for the Millennium

http://millennium.sonymusic.com

Our friends at Sony have compiled music from nearly five hundred artists representing every genre. Sit back, relax, and enjoy.

551 *Yellow Submarine*

http://www.hollywoodandvine.com/yellowsubmarine

Everyone can enjoy this site that celebrates the release of the remastered versions of the famous Beatles animated movie and music soundtrack.

552 Everything Music

http://music.yahoo.com
http://www.ubl.com

Type in an artist, album, or song, and you will get detailed information about your selection.

553 Concerts and More

http://www.pollstar.com
http://www.tourdates.com
http://www.enspot.com

If you want to attend a concert, these are your sites to find out who is appearing where and when.

554 Music on the Net

http://www.rockonthenet.com

This is a great site that will keep you informed about musicians and groups.

555 *Rolling Stone*

http://www.rollingstone.com

This magazine has been reporting on music forever.

556 Rock and Roll Hall of Fame

http://www.rockhall.com

The Net rocks at the Rock and Roll Hall of Fame.

557 Music Lyrics

http://www.lyrics.ch

This site has an inventory of the words to over one hundred thousand songs.

558 Country Music

http://www.countrycool.com
http://www.musiccountry.com

It's the most popular music in the U.S. If you like it, you'll not want to miss this site.

559 Surfin' in Margaritaville

http://www.margaritaville.com

Thanks to Jimmy Buffett, you can surf and listen to great music here.

560 **Can't Find That Station**

http://www.radioguide.com/cities.html
http://www.radio-locator.com
http://www.publicradiofan.com

Every time you visit a new city, you probably have to fumble around to find the radio stations that you like. Well, here are the complete listings in the U.S.

561 **Name That Tune**

http://www.starcd.com
http://www.emarker.com

Have you ever heard a song on the radio but can't name it? Your problem is solved. These sites provide the playlists for many major cities.

562 **CDs Galore**

http://www.cdnow.com
http://www.cduniverse.com

If you like music, check out these sites. Find your favorite performer, and listen to clips from the album. Try before you buy.

>> *News*

563 **News as Easy as 1, 2, 3**

http://www.msnbc.com
http://www.abcnews.com
http://www.cbsnews.com

Get your news directly from the sites of the "big three" television networks.

117

564 ## CNN and CNNfn

http://www.cnn.com

http://www.cnnfn.com

http://my.cnn.com

Here is up-to-date news and financial information from the CNN group.

565 ## Weekly News

http://www.time.com

http://www.newsweek.com

http://www.usnews.com

It's time for your weekly news from *TIME*, *Newsweek*, and *U.S. News & World Report*.

566 ## Anchors Good-bye

http://www.ananova.com

Late-breaking news: Ananova replaces Peter, Tom, and Dan. Complete details are available online.

567 ## Desktop News

http://www.desktopnews.com

http://www.entrypoint.com

Keep up-to-date with financial and business news, sports, entertainment, and more on your desktop.

568 ## Knowledgeable Reader

http://www.newswatch.org

http://www.mediachannel.org

These sites have analysis of current events that might shed some light for you on world happenings.

569 **Media Information**

http://www.poynter.org/medianews

Read about interesting news stories from several major publications.

570 **Newspapers Everywhere**

http://www.thepaperboy.com
http://www.worldnews.com
http://www.newslink.org
http://www.all-links.com/newscentral

There are many great newspapers on the Net. Find them at these sites.

571 **A Lot of News**

http://www.totalnews.com

Total News contains many major publications with a lot of links to great news, sports, entertainment, and opinion sites, and an interesting search capability.

572 **Newspaper Heaven**

http://www.nytimes.com
http://www.usatoday.com
http://www.latimes.com
http://www.washingtonpost.com

Cuddle up to the screen and read to your heart's content.

573 **Hot off the Press**

http://www.nytimes.com/aponline

News updates are available every ten minutes at *The New York Times* on the Web.

My Newspaper.com

http://www.crayon.net

Create your own newspaper. However, you'll have to provide your own coffee.

 ### Your News Outlet

http://www.newshub.com

In one location, receive timely news stories from many of the finest publications on the Net. You can even customize the site for your own needs.

 ### Be an Individual

http://www.individual.com

These folks have been around awhile, providing customizable news and information.

 ### Headline News

http://www.headlinespot.com
http://www.headlinenews.com
http://www.7am.com
http://www.1stheadlines.com

Browse the headlines, and get your news quickly and easily at these sites.

 ### Brief News on Your Desktop

http://www.msnbc.com/toolkit.asp

Let MSNBC "push" news and information to your desktop. It provides brief summaries of a variety of stories and features. If a particular item interests you, click on it and go directly to the Web site.

579 Reuters

http://www.reuters.com

Many publications receive their information from Reuters. Now, you can get it right from the horse's mouth.

580 Good News

http://www.positivepress.com
http://www.goodnewsnetwork.org

Tired of predominantly negative news reporting? Read the positive news here.

581 Random Acts of Kindness

http://www.actsofkindness.org

Its goal is to promote and publicize, in a wide variety of ways, the extraordinary power and importance of simple human kindness.

582 The Electronic Library

http://www.elibrary.com
http://www.newstrawler.com

These sites let you search for items that have been in articles in magazines, newspapers, and more.

583 A Garage of Gems

http://www.garage.com/geoffsGems.shtml
http://www.tomalak.org

Every weekday, Geoff and Lawrence will e-mail you links to the day's best high-tech news from a variety of major business publications.

A World of Information

http://www.worldskip.com

From every country in the world, you'll find news, information, products, services, and more.

>> Newsletters

 ### Push It to Me

http://www.infobeat.com
http://home.netscape.com/ibd/index.html

You name it, and these companies will provide it to you—sports, news, weather, Internet information, stocks, and more. Push (delivery) technology is the way to go, and these services lead the pack.

 ### Lots of Topics

http://www.fidget.com
http://www.webscoutlists.com
http://www.topica.com

Every interest group under the sun can be found here. Subscribe to a newsletter of interest to you.

 ### Daily E-Mail Tips

http://www.elementkjournals.com/zdtips
http://www.dummiesdaily.com

If you want to get a tip a day for many software products, visit these sites.

 ### Here's a Tip

http://www.tipworld.com

Name the topic and TipWorld has a newsletter for you. Enjoy the tips.

589 Daily Tip

http://www.cybertip4theday.com

Receive a daily tip. From autos to travel, you can subscribe to many different cybertips.

590 Wired for Information

http://www.backwire.com

Backwire offers, for free, over thirty newsletters covering many different topics.

591 Zooba?

http://www.zooba.com

Receive easy-to-read e-mail about more than forty subject areas. From biography to travel, you'll enjoy these simple but informative Zooba mailings.

>> Outdoor Life

592 Park Central

http://www.llbean.com/parksearch
http://www.recreation.gov
http://www.nps.gov

Thank you, L.L. Bean and the U.S. government. These sites have over one thousand USA parks in their database.

593 Ski Mt. Everest

http://www.everest.simobil.si

On October 17, 2000, Davo Karnicar accomplished an uninterrupted ski descent from the top of the world's highest mountain. You can read all about it and even watch a video of it.

594   ## Resort Sports Network

http://www.rsn.com

If you love the outdoors, you will want to check out the beautiful camera shots of these resorts.

595   ## Be Adventurous

http://www.adventuresports.com

If having the wind in your face and your heart in your throat is what makes you feel alive, then this is the place for you.

596   ## Adrenaline Online

http://www.extremesports.com

Extreme sports are not for me to play, but I love watching them. Either way, you'll enjoy this site.

597   ## Go to the Mountain

http://www.mountainzone.com

For skiing, snowboarding, biking, hiking, climbing, and even photography, go to the mountain.

598   ## Hunting and Fishing

http://www.spav.com

This site is dedicated to the fishing and hunting enthusiasts around the world.

599   ## The Outdoor Life

http://www.alloutdoors.com
http://www.outdoor.com
http://www.fishsearch.com

Hunting, fishing, and a lot more are here for you.

600 Let's Go Huntin'

http://www.hunting.net

This site has a directory of over 1,500 outfitters and lodges, information on all types of game, and a lot of other stuff.

601 Goin' Campin'

http://www.campnetamerica.com

Have fun, and don't forget to pack this site as part of your equipment.

602 *Outside* Online

http://www.outsidemag.com

This site is invigorating. It might even tempt you to get offline and go outside.

603 Serious Sports

http://www.serioussports.com

You'll find information here about: hang gliding, paragliding, skydiving, soaring, Western ranches, horsepacking, rock climbing, mountaineering, fishing, whitewater rafting and kayaking, sea kayaking, outdoor schools, and more.

604 Got Equipment?

http://www.rei.com
http://www.galyans.com
http://www.greatoutdoors.com

If you're an outdoorsman, you have to have the right stuff. These stores will keep you well equipped.

>> *People*

 Six Billion . . .

> http://www.popexpo.net
> http://www.pbs.org/sixbillion
> http://www.prb.org
> http://www.census.gov/cgi-bin/popclock

> . . . and counting. Find out lots of interesting details about the world's population.

 For People Who Need People

> http://people.aol.com/people

> Keep up to date about people—the famous ones, that is.

 People Spot

> http://www.peoplespot.com

> From learning about notable people to connecting with others on the Net, this is the perfect spot for inquiring minds.

 Biography

> http://www.biography.com

> *Biography* on A&E is an excellent show. This site has a searchable database of more than 25,000 famous people.

Historical Biographies

> http://www.s9.com/biography

> There are over twenty-eight thousand searchable historical figures at this site. Make sure you don't miss taking the Master Biographer Challenge.

610 ## Biography 101

http://www.amillionlives.com

If your bookshelf is filled with biographies, you'll enjoy this professional collection of biographical Web sites.

611 ## Presidential Biographies

http://www.ipl.org/ref/POTUS

They are all here, from Washington to the current occupant of the White House.

612 ## Women Rule the World

http://www.firstladies.org
http://www.greatwomen.org

Let's face it, women rule the roost. Check out all the first ladies and the National Women's Hall of Fame.

613 ## Stamp History

http://www.stamponhistory.com

This site explores the lives of important historical people through their pictures on postage stamps.

614 ## The Nobel Prize

http://www.nobel.se

See all of the winners of the Nobel Prize in medicine since 1901.

615 ## Incredible People

http://etext.virginia.edu/jefferson
http://www.westegg.com/einstein
http://edison.rutgers.edu
http://www.pathfinder.com/time/time100/poc/home.html

Thomas Jefferson, Albert Einstein, and Thomas Edison are three who have truly made a difference.

616 Benjamin Franklin

http://www.fi.edu/TOC.franklin.html

If you ever need to do a report on Benjamin Franklin or just want to know more about the man on the one-hundred-dollar bill, this site will do it.

617 Abraham Lincoln

http://www.netins.net/showcase/creative/lincoln.html

Honest Abe has been done proud at this site. There are tons of resources here.

618 Overachiever

http://www.achievement.org
http://www.greatachievements.org

This site features people who have been successful in business, the arts, entertainment, sports, and more. Learn about the most important individuals and events of the twentieth century.

619 Dollar Bill

http://www.microsoft.com/BillGates
http://www.quuxuum.org/~evan/bgnw.html
http://www.usnews.com/usnews/nycu/tech/billgate/gatehigh.htm

Love him or not, Bill Gates has had a major impact on most of us. Here's his Web site, his net worth, and—best of all—a tour of his 66,000 square foot house.

620 Influential Folks

http://www.time.com/time/time100

TIME magazine has covered most of the influential people of the 20th century at this site.

621 **Wealth Meter**

http://www.cnetinvestor.com/ceometer/ceometer.asp

We're obsessed with the earnings of the superrich. At this interactive site, find out which billionaires made or lost money today.

622 *Forbes* **400**

http://www.forbes.com/tool/toolbox/rich400

Check out a list of the richest people in America.

623 **Happy Birthday**

http://www.anybirthday.com
http://www.famousbirthdays.com
http://www.scopesys.com/anyday
http://www.440.com/twtd/today.html
http://www.historychannel.com/thisday
http://www.thehistorynet.com/today/today.htm

Who was born? Who died? And what else happened on this day? Find out here.

624 **Wills and Graves of the Rich and Famous**

http://www.ca-probate.com/wills.htm
http://www.findagrave.com

Not to be too morbid, but these sites have a lot of interesting information.

625 **Four Legends**

http://www.dilbert.com
http://www.marthastewart.com
http://www.elvis.com
http://www.sinatra.com

Dilbert, Martha, Elvis, and Frank . . . they have not left the Net.

626 Unique and Magnifique

http://www.threestooges.com
http://www.whyaduck.com
http://www.oprah.com

The Three Stooges, the Marx Brothers, and Oprah have all become legends in their respective fields.

627 Multiculturalism

http://curry.edschool.virginia.edu/go/multicultural

Multiculturalism has become a major part of our education system and schools' curricula. Read and learn all about it here.

628 Matchmaker, Matchmaker . . .

http://www.match.com
http://www.2ofaKind.com

If Yenta knew about these dating sites, she'd be singing, "The times, they are a changin'."

629 Class Reunion

http://www.classmates.com

Looking for your former classmates? You may find them here. Enter your name, year of graduation, and high school.

>> Pets

630 Your Guide to Pets on the Net

http://www.acmepet.com

You can tell that they love pets at this site.

631 **Pleasant Planet**

http://www.petplanet.com

Pets make great family members. If you already have a pet, or are considering one, these sites will be great resources.

632 **PetTalk America**

http://www.pettalk.com

Listen to Bob Vella's nationally syndicated radio show, chat with other pet lovers, learn more about your pet, and check out his Q&A section.

633 **Pet Experts**

http://www.petcity.com

Got a question about one of your pets? Go to the city, they'll have the answer.

634 **Animal Farm**

http://www.animalfair.com

This site says, "We're dedicated to a vital and enriching bond between humans and animals. Our mission is to present some hip, broad-ranging and entertaining content about pets, animals, and people who love them—from the ordinary to the extraordinary."

635 **Allpets**

http://www.allpets.com

Humans need a PetCyclopedia with such interesting categories as "Single Pet People" and "Pet Flicks." All the major pets have their own sections.

636 The Animal Network

http://www.animalnetwork.com
http://www.allpets.com

Cats, dogs, fish, reptiles, horses, and more are here.

637 Got Information?

http://www.pet-net.net

Whether you're looking for fellow pet enthusiasts, information about care, breeders, or pet supplies, you're sure to find it here. They'll even design a pet Web site for you.

638 Pet Heroes

http://www.petheroes.com

Ilonka Sjak-Shie has been kind enough to develop this online pet community, which unites pet lovers from all over the world and demonstrates that every pet is a hero.

639 Keep That Pet Healthy

http://www.healthypet.com

Now that you have found your pet, here's a site that will help you keep it healthy.

640 Animal Sounds

http://www.georgetown.edu/cball/animals/animals.html

And you thought animals all over the world sound the same? Find out how different they can be.

641 It's Raining Cats and Dogs

http://www.canismajor.com/dog
http://www.purina.com
http://dogs.about.com

Before you go out and buy that cuddly puppy or furry kitten, make sure you do a little research. These sites tell a lot about these great pets.

642 Dog House

http://www.doghause.com

No doubt, you'll want to stay in this doghouse for a long time.

643 All about Cats

http://cats.about.com

From adoption to literature and art, these folks have lots of good feline things for you.

644 Horse Sense

http://www.haynet.net
http://www.horse-country.com

These are great resources for horse lovers—sites, sites, and more sites to visit. Jump right over.

645 Travel Companion

http://www.travelpets.com
http://www.petswelcome.com
http://www.petvacations.com
http://www.petsonthego.com
http://www.travelingdogs.com
http://www.companimalz.com
http://www.dogfriendly.com

Don't leave home without them. Before you hit the road, read about pet-friendly accommodations.

>> *Politics*

 Political Portals

http://www.politics.com
http://politics.yahoo.com
http://www.opensecrets.org
http://www.e-thepeople.com
http://www.freedomchannel.com
http://www.campaignline.com/odds

Keep up with campaigns and other political developments through these sites.

 Politics on the Net

http://www.politicalresources.net

This contains political sites from around the globe. View the map, and click the particular part of the world that interests you.

 Grass Roots Initiative

http://www.grassroots.com

This political network is designed to help make the political process more accessible to everyone.

 Political Junkies

http://www.allpolitics.com
http://www.speakout.com

If you love politics, you shouldn't miss these sites. You'll find timely news and issues discussed here.

650 ## Smart Voter

http://www.vote-smart.org

http://www.congress.org

Track the performance of over thirteen thousand political leaders, and write your own individual congressman at congress.org.

651 ## The Buck Stops Here

http://www.tray.com/fecinfo

http://www.crp.org

These are places to discover who gave what to which political candidates.

652 ## Let's Party

http://www.rnc.org

http://www.democrats.org

http://www.reformparty.org

Visit the official Web sites for the Republican, Democrat and Reform parties.

653 ## The Great Debate

http://www.mbcnet.org/debateweb

Enjoy watching the actual presidential debates dating back to 1960.

654 ## Electoral College

http://www.jump.net/~jnhtx/ec/ec.html

Every four years, we hear a lot about the electoral college. This site lets you "play" with components of the electoral process. Pick a winner in each state and see what happens.

History of Presidential Elections

http://www.multied.com/elections
http://election2000.stanford.edu

From 1789 to 2000, you'll find interesting election information and results.

Gone Forever

http://www.politicalgraveyard.com

Our politicians have taxed us to death. Now thanks to Lawrence Kestenbaum, you will know the final resting places of over thirty thousand politicians.

Watergate

http://www.lib.berkeley.edu/MRC/watergate.html
http://www.nara.gov/nixon/tapes/index.html

It's an infamous name that will be with us forever. Read about Watergate and listen to many of the recordings online. There are approximately 3,700 hours of tapes.

Political Cartoons

http://www.politicalcartoons.com
http://www.politicalcartoons.com/teacher

Enjoy timely political cartoons at these sites.

Dr. Seuss Goes to War

http://orpheus.ucsd.edu/speccoll/dspolitic

Dr. Seuss was not known for his political cartoons. Now you can view more than four hundred of them here.

>> *Privacy*

660 ### Internet Cookies

http://www.cookiecentral.com

As you surf, cookies are stored on your computer. Learn all about Internet cookies here.

661 ### Privacy on the Net

http://www.privacyrights.org
http://www.privacy.net
http://www.ftc.gov/kidzprivacy

Concerned about privacy? Get acquainted with the issues here.

662 ### Privacy Center

http://www.epic.org

This organization was established in 1994 to focus public attention on emerging civil liberties issues and to protect privacy, the First Amendment, and constitutional values. See the latest news here.

663 ### Be Anonymous

https://www.safeweb.com
http://www.anonymizer.com
http://www.enonymous.com

Web sites can track you while you surf. Find out how to surf anonymously, and learn a lot about privacy issues on the Net.

"This is the finest, most comprehensive, and informative term paper I've ever read. But you were supposed to write about 'Plato' not 'Play-Doh'."

>> *Psychology & Philosophy*

 ### The Platinum Rule

http://www.platinumrule.com

Everyone knows the golden rule: "Do unto others as you would have them do unto you." The real key to success may be to apply the Platinum Rule: "Do unto others as they would like done unto them!"

 ### Take the Test

http://www.davideck.com
http://www.emode.com

Go to this site for a variety of evaluations, including IQ and personality tests.

 ### Affirmative Parenting?

http://www.rosemond.com

I enjoy John Rosemond's perspective, and I hope you will too. His parental advice is straightforward and makes a lot of sense.

 ### Log Off!

http://www.netaddiction.com
http://www.netaddiction.com/resources/test.htm

Are you spending too much time on the Net? Take the test and get some advice.

668 ## Psychology

http://www.thepsych.com

Sign up for Psych 101 here.

669 ## Philosophy on the Net

http://www.utm.edu/research/iep

Ponder the big issues at The Internet Encyclopedia of Philosophy.

>> Publications, Business & Financial

670 ## American City Business Journals

http://www.bizjournals.com

This site has major business publications from over forty cities.

671 ## Dow Jones and Company

http://www.wsj.com
http://www.barrons.com

You'll be in good company with these publications that provide in-depth business reporting.

672 ## Let's Talk about Business

http://www.inc.com
http://www.forbes.com
http://www.fortune.com
http://www.businessweek.com

It's not exactly business as usual here. These offline publications excel on the Net.

Money Talks

http://www.smartmoney.com
http://www.savewealth.com

Be smart; use your money wisely, and save your wealth for retirement.

 Financial Reporting

http://www.worth.com
http://www.economist.com
http://www.bloomberg.com
http://www.kiplinger.com

Some of the best financial reporting offline is also on the Net.

 Your Path to *Money*

http://www.money.com

Money magazine provides this very comprehensive financial site.

>> *Publications, General*

 Magazines Galore

http://www.enews.com
http://www.magportal.com

If you want to find a magazine or article on the Net, it will probably be here.

 Magazine Links

http://ajr.newslink.org/mag.html

Which magazines have the largest circulation? You'll find the answer here. Many of these publications are online. Happy reading.

678 Magazine Newsstand

http://www.magazine-rack.com

Want to read a magazine? This newsstand lists many popular ones by category.

679 Upscale Magazines

http://www.newyorker.com
http://www.theatlantic.com
http://www.harpers.org

Though *Harper*'s content is not actually online, click on "Harper's Index" to be instantly propelled to hundreds of interesting statistics.

680 The Farmer's Almanac

http://www.almanac.com

It's the one and only.

681 The S-Word

http://www.slate.com
http://www.salon.com

Slate and *Salon* are two thought-provoking online publications that will entertain and move you.

682 I've Got a Secret

http://www.bottomlinesecrets.com

If you want some very good tips about health, wealth, travel, business, life, and people, visit here.

683 Find an Article

http://www.findarticles.com

Need to find an article? Use this site to search for quality articles in more than three hundred magazines and journals.

684 **Dredging Up Drudge**

http://www.drudgereport.com

Remember Matt Drudge? He broke the Monica Lewinsky story. Beyond his late-breaking news, he does have some good resources for you.

>> *Quotes*

 685 **Famous Quotes**

http://www.bartleby.com/100
http://www.quotationspage.com
http://www.aphorismsgalore.com

You can find most of them here. You can quote me on that.

 686 **Quoteland**

http://www.quoteland.com
http://www.quotations.co.uk

Many of life's truths come from these quotations.

 687 **E-Mail That Quote**

http://www.quoteworld.org

Receive an e-mail every day with a new quote. The site sports over fourteen thousand interesting ones.

 688 **Spockisms**

http://www.cs.ubc.ca/cgi-bin/nph-spock

Ah, the sage advice of Mr. Spock. Here's a simple site that provides quotes from Star Trek's famous Vulcan philosopher.

"My history professor told me to use the Internet for research, and it's been very helpful. I've located seventeen people who have offered to sell me a term paper!"

>> Reference & Research

 ### 689 Reference Desk

http://www.refdesk.com
http://www.referencedesk.org

Each of these sites states that it is "the best source" on the Net. No doubt, you will find many incredible sites at both. Plan on staying for a while.

 ### 690 I'm Busy

http://www.ceoexpress.com

Patricia Pomerleau says, "As a senior executive, I have found my peers to be busy people with little time or patience for the Internet. The sheer volume of information and extensive time it can take to locate useful sites can be a significant deterrent for executives interested in using the Web." Here's the solution.

 ### 691 Journalist's Resource Guide

http://www.journalismnet.com

A journalist has created a site that will assist in finding or searching anything on the Net.

692 Information at Your Fingertips

http://info-s.com

This site has over seventy thousand links. It is well organized and will probably provide you with a world of good information. Take it for a spin and get acquainted.

693 About Mining

http://about.com

Over seven hundred guides with a passion for the Internet will lead you to interesting articles and sites. From the arts to TV, you will find some golden sites here, so get your shovel and dig in.

694 All About the Net

http://azlist.about.com

Here is a listing of guide topics in alphabetical order, so you'll never be lost again.

695 It's All 4 You

http://www.4anything.com

The name says it best: "4anything" on the Net, you should visit here.

696 Daily Internet Features

http://www.yil.com

It's an *Internet Life*. Daily, this publication will e-mail to you: the Net Buzz, a Radio Site of the Day, a Useful Site of the Day, and much more.

697 Resources Galore

http://www.eblast.com
http://www.infoplease.com
http://www.beaucoup.com

Looking for something on the Net? These are good sites to find almost anything.

698 Research It!

http://www.itools.com/research-it

If you seek something on the subjects of language, geography, finance, shipping and mailing, famous quotes, or other, check out this worthwhile site.

699 Cross Reference

http://www.xrefer.com

Search for information that is in encyclopedias, dictionaries, thesauri, and books of quotations from the world's leading publishers.

700 It's a Fact

http://www.factmonster.com

This "monster" has essential reference materials, fun facts and features, and homework help in an environment designed for kids.

701 Look Smart

http://www.looksmart.com

You'll look smart after visiting here. Name it, and this place has the information.

Why?

http://www.whyfiles.org

Do you frequently ask "why?" If so, go to the Why Files. You'll be happy you did, and don't ask me why!

 I Know You!

http://www.knowx.com

http://www.ussearch.com

These sites bring public records to the general public. There will be a small fee for the search.

>> Safe Surfing

 Trash on the Net

http://www.surfcontrol.com

http://www.netnanny.com

These sites have software products that can help keep the bad stuff off your computer screen.

 Be Safe

http://www.safekids.com

Use this site to identify safety concerns and to formulate a plan for your family.

 Teen Safety

http://parentnewsnet.com/safety.shtml

Teens need to learn how to be safe online. Here's a good resource with a guideline for parents, too.

707 **Surfing the Net with Kids**

http://www.surfnetkids.com

Barbara Feldman, a columnist, has interesting things for kids to do on the Net. Make sure you sign up for her weekly newsletter.

708 **Family Friendly**

http://www.virtuocity.com/family/Index.cfm

Search for family friendly sites from this location. Just about any area of interest is covered.

709 **It's a Kid's World**

http://www.pbskids.org
http://kidexchange.about.com

This one will be sure to delight kids and teens. It has interesting sites, changes on a regular basis, and has educational information such as "kid science."

710 **Lycos and AOL Know Kids**

http://www.lycoszone.com
http://www.aol.com/netfind/kids

Lycos and AOL make it easier for kids on the Net.

>> *Science*

711 **$E=mc^2$**

http://www.westegg.com/einstein
http://www.aip.org/history/einstein

Here's everything you ever wanted to know (and maybe more) about Albert Einstein.

712 **Physics is Fun**

http://www.physlink.com

That's what this site says as it examines such things as how yo-yos work. Some good cartoons are also provided.

713 **Fun with Pfizer**

http://www.pfizerfunzone.com

The FunZone encourages kids and their teachers to participate in and enjoy the world of science.

714 **Science Online**

http://www.scitechdaily.com
http://www.scienceagogo.com

It's educational, fun, and even interesting. Here you can read many timely stories about science.

715 **Science Resource Guide**

http://www.sciencegems.com

Frank and Jim have categorized more than fourteen thousand science sites. These guys are true gems.

716 **The Science Learning Network**

http://www.sln.org
http://www.extremescience.com

How do you make science a really great learning experience—fun, easy, and informative? These sites pass the test.

717 **Yucky Sites for Kids**

http://www.yucky.com

Here's a great place for science information and fun.

718 **Mad Science**

http://www.madsci.org

MadSci Network calls itself "a collective cranium of scientists providing their answers to your questions."

719 **Junk Science**

http://www.junkscience.com

I know it's hard to believe that anyone would try to fool us about scientific studies, but I promise you it happens. Don't be fooled again.

720 **The Last Word**

http://www.last-word.com

How does a potato-powered clock work? Find out at this site. There are over 450 answers to a lot of interesting questions.

721 **The Final Frontier**

http://www.space.com
http://www.spaceref.com
http://www.spacestation.com
http://www.astronomy.com

These sites can be considered the next best things to being out there.

722 **Space News**

http://space.popsci.com/space

Get your current space news here.

723 **Star Gazing**

http://www.wunderground.com/sky

Enter your zip code, and you will be propelled into outer space.

724 ## StarChild

http://starchild.gsfc.nasa.gov

The StarChild site is a service of the High Energy Astrophysics Science Archive Research Center (HEASARC). I promise this site is a lot easier to use than the name implies. This is a great site to learn about our solar system, universe, and other space stuff.

725 ## Next Stop . . .

http://www.mars2030.net

. . . Mars!

726 ## Science Surf

http://www.williamcalvin.com

William H. Calvin, teacher and author, maintains this excellent science site with links to many other mind-expanding locations.

727 ## The Wizard's Lab

http://library.advanced.org/11924

Learn about motion, sound, light, energy, electricity, and magnetism at this fun site. You'll want to take the quiz and find out more.

728 ## Institute of Human Origins

http://www.asu.edu/clas/iho
http://www.mnh.si.edu/anthro/humanorigins

Explore our origins. Plan on spending eons here.

Interactive Frog Dissection

http://curry.edschool.virginia.edu/go/frog/menu.html

This lab activity will help you learn the anatomy of a frog and also provide a better understanding of the anatomy of vertebrates, including humans.

NASA in Cyberspace

http://www.nasa.gov

http://nasatechnology.nasa.gov

NASA is hip to your needs. It even has an area titled, "Cool NASA Websites."

NASA's New Frontiers

http://marsweb.jpl.nasa.gov

http://spaceflight.nasa.gov

NASA is firmly committed to spreading knowledge acquired from its research. Check out the Mars and International Space Station Web sites; they're out of sight.

The Ocean

http://topex-www.jpl.nasa.gov

This project is for understanding our oceans and climate, and it is done from space!

Windows to the Universe

http://www.earthsky.com

http://www.windows.umich.edu

When it comes to understanding our earth and universe, these sites will inform and entertain you.

734 Earthquakes

http://www.crustal.ucsb.edu/ics/understanding

Take a quiz and learn a lot about earthquakes at this site.

735 Volcano World

http://volcano.und.nodak.edu
http://vulcan.wr.usgs.gov

If it has anything to do with volcanoes, you will find it here.

736 Dinosaur-o-mania

http://www.fmnh.org/sue
http://www.dinoheart.org
http://www.dinosauricon.com
http://www.zoomdinosaurs.com
http://palaeo.gly.bris.ac.uk/dinobase/dinopage.html

Everybody loves dinosaurs, so zoom over to the society. Get lots of information and check out the links page.

737 The Human Anatomy

http://www.innerbody.com
http://www.ehc.com/vbody.asp

Get ready to find a lot of pictures and descriptive information about the body.

738 Elusive Illusions

http://www.illusionworks.com
http://www.sandlotscience.com

Is it real, or is it an illusion? Spend a few moments here for some scientific fun.

"My team is developing the world's greatest search engine. We've used it to find Kate's contact lens, Larry's ambition, and your hair!"

>> *Search Engines*

 739 ### Search Engine Watch

http://www.searchenginewatch.com
http://www.searchengineshowdown.com

These sites are designed for serious searchers, Webmasters, marketers and others who love search engines.

 740 ### Excited About Searchin'

http://www.netscape.com
http://www.excite.com
http://www.lycos.com
http://www.yahoo.com
http://www.altavista.com

These early search engines offer many interesting and exciting features.

 741 ### Go Get Hot

http://www.go.com
http://www.hotbot.com

It seems you can't have too many search engines. These are two popular spots.

(742) Search Alternatives

http://www.dogpile.com
http://www.northernlight.com
http://www.profusion.com
http://www.mamma.com

Let's face it, searching for stuff on the Net can be difficult. These sites might make it a little easier.

(743) Fast Search

http://www.google.com
http://www.alltheweb.com
http://www.allonesearch.com

The Web is getting huge, and we need fast, efficient tools to find things. Here are some search engines that are ready for the task.

(744) Search A to Z

http://www.searchenginesgalore.com
http://www.searchability.com

Here are search engines for every topic available.

(745) The Internet Sleuth

http://www.searchbug.com

This site will search hundreds of different databases for you. It even ranks the most popular types of searches.

(746) C Net's Search

http://www.search.com

It isn't called Search.com for nothing. This will help you find any number of things on the Net.

747 Simply Elegant

http://www.simpli.com

Here's a very powerful search engine that has been beautifully designed.

748 Coping with Searching

http://www.copernic.com

The existence of over a billion Web pages and search engines that yield useless information can indeed be infuriating. This search alternative can help solve these problems.

749 Top Fifty

http://50.lycos.com
http://buzz.yahoo.com

What are people searching for? Lycos and Yahoo! can tell you. It's a good window into pop culture and current events.

750 Ask Jeeves, and He'll Find It

http://www.askjeeves.com

You simply ask Jeeves a question, and he will find the correct answer for you. Most of the time, he is right on target. He can also find things you never would have thought of. Amazing!

751 Family Friendly

http://www.ajkids.com
http://www.familyfriendlysearch.com

Need a search engine that kids can use? These sites meet the challenge.

Smart Searching

http://www.searchopolis.com

Searchopolis is a good search engine that has been designed for students.

 Find an Old Friend (or a New One)

http://people.yahoo.com
http://www.whowhere.lycos.com
http://www.theultimates.com
http://www.bigfoot.com
http://www.switchboard.com

Find anyone's phone number or e-mail address by using these information search engines.

754 **Phone Number = Name and Address**

http://www.anywho.com
http://www.anywho.com/telq.html

Do you have a phone number but don't have the corresponding name or address? With this site, you can have it all.

755 **World Wide Phone Numbers**

http://www.phonenumbers.net

From Argentina to Zimbabwe, you'll have telephone numbers at your fingertips.

 The Ultimate Guide . . .

http://www.infospace.com

. . . to find people, places, or things can be found here.

757 **Area Code Search**

http://decoder.americom.com

Plug in an area code, and you will learn which city it belongs to. Or, enter a certain city name to find out its area code(s).

758 **Zip Code Lookup**

http://www.westminster.ca/cdnlook.htm

http://www.usps.gov/ncsc/welcome1.htm

Do you need to know the zip code for an address? This is the location.

759 **My, Oh My**

http://my.netscape.com

http://my.yahoo.com

http://my.excite.com

http://my.snap.com

Get all your news and information from one Web page: You can even customize it for your own needs. Make sure you use one for your "start page."

760 **International Search Engines**

http://www.searchenginecolossus.com

Join the World Wide Web and go international. This site has search engines for every country.

761 **Internet Robot**

http://www.botspot.com

On the Net, there are robots that are happy to do the searching for you. This site lists the best of the "bots."

762 ## Cyndi's List

http://www.CyndisList.com

When it comes to genealogy, Cyndi's list is quite complete. She has more than eighty thousand links related to the subject.

763 ## Ancestors

http://www.ancestry.com
http://www.rootsweb.com
http://www.familysearch.org
http://www.genealogy.com
http://www.genealogytoday.com
http://www.genealogyportal.com

Want to know about your past? These genealogy sites will keep you busy.

764 ## Genealogy

http://www.usgenweb.org
http://www.ngsgenealogy.org
http://www.familytreemaker.com
http://www.genealogytoolbox.com

Genealogy is one of today's most popular hobbies. Use these sites to help research your ancestors.

765 ## Find Me

http://www.search-shark.com
http://members.aa.net/~flip/search/search.html

If someone can be found, this shark will put the bite on him.

766 ## Internet Tour

http://www.etour.com

Are you tired of searching on your own for things on the Internet? Would you like a tour guide? Etour will be happy to take you on one. Best of all, it's free.

>> *Seniors*

 ### AARP Webplace

http://www.aarp.org

With more than 30 million members, AARP is the nation's largest organization for ages fifty and up. Learn about computers, the Internet, legislative issues important to seniors, legal help, travel and leisure activities, personal finance, and more.

768 ### Retirement Sounds Good

http://www.asec.org/toolshm.htm

Start preparing long before you retire. Over thirty percent of Americans have not put money aside for their golden years. Don't be one of them.

769 ### Fifty Something

http://www.thirdage.com

ThirdAge is a site that addresses the needs and concerns of the baby boomer generation. If that's you, this might be a good place for you to hang out.

 ### Mr. Long-Term Care

http://www.mr-longtermcare.com

The following testimonial says it best: "I want to thank Mr. Long-Term Care for his commitment to improving long-term care and to educating the public about the great need for affordable quality care in this country." —Hillary Rodham Clinton.

>> Shipping

 Postage.com

http://www.stamps.com

http://www.estamp.com

Tired of waiting in long lines at the post office? Now you can use your computer as a postage meter. Download some software, and you'll be ready to go.

 Package Tracking with UPS and FedEx

http://www.ups.com/tracking/tracking.html

http://www.fedex.com/us/tracking

Track a package that was sent via UPS or FedEx.

 Track Any Package

http://www.packtrack.com

Here's a site that allows you to track a package sent through the major delivery services. If you do a lot of shipping, you should place this one on your browser toolbar.

>> Shopping

 Shop Safely

http://www.safeshopping.org

http://www.truste.org

http://www.bbbonline.org

The Internet is the world's largest shopping mall, and these sites should help you become a more knowledgeable online consumer.

775 Smart Consumer

http://www.bizrate.com

http://www.esmarts.com

Be a sharp consumer. These sites offer information, Web sites, and a weekly newsletter with various shopping categories.

776 Everything is Negotiable

http://www.haggle.com

Do you enjoy bargaining? Go ahead, enter the Haggle zone, online.

777 Shopping with a Cause

http://www.greatergood.com

GreaterGood allows you to shop online and have a portion of the proceeds go to a charitable cause.

778 Catalogs and More

http://www.catalogcity.com

http://www.catalogsite.com

Are you a catalog shopper? If so, these sites are sure to delight.

779 Shop Online

http://www.shoponline123.com

This offline publishing company has rated hundreds of online shopping sites for you.

780 Shop 'Til You Drop

http://www.buy.com

http://www.shoppingspot.com

http://www.reallybigmall.com

Shopping on the Internet has become very popular, and these sites have tons of items for you to buy.

Outlet Store

http://www.bluefly.com

Bluefly is one of the original online stores on the Net. You'll be sure to find some good deals here.

 Professional Bargain Shopper

http://www.dealtime.com
http://www.mysimon.com
http://www.pricescan.com

Wouldn't it be great to have your very own personal shopper who knows exactly where to get the best deals? Here are some good ones, and you don't have to pay for the service.

 Coupons Galore

http://www.hotcoupons.com
http://www.valpak.com
http://www.valupage.com
http://www.supercoups.com
http://www.mycoupons.com
http://www.coolsavings.com

If you're a coupon clipper, you'll love getting these coupons on the Net.

As Seen on TV

http://www.asotv.com

Here's a potpourri of special things you can buy online, from books to greeting cards to things you've seen on infomercials on TV.

Gift Certificate

http://www.giftcertificates.com

Send someone a gift certificate from one of many name brand companies.

786 **Gift Registration**

http://www.webistry.com

How would you like to be able to conveniently inform your family and friends all over the world what gifts you want to receive? Register here.

787 **I Wish**

http://www.ugive.com

http://www.wishbox.com

Let these sites assist in both the gift giving and receiving processes.

788 **What a Deal!**

http://www.bargaindog.com

http://www.salescircular.com

We all love deals. These sites will help you find the best deals on and off the Net.

789 **Off-Line Sales**

http://www.saleshound.com

Where are the sales and good deals in the "bricks and mortar" world of the stores? Pop in your zip code, and you'll know where the sales are.

790 **Hey Big Spender**

http://www.luxuryfinder.com

If you've got big bucks, visit the LuxuryFinder site and spend away.

Flower Power

http://www.proflowers.com
http://www.1800flowers.com

Flowers always brighten up a room. Here are some companies who will be happy to send them on a regular basis.

 Sports Equipment

http://www.fogdog.com
http://www.mvp.com

Buy any sports item online.

>> *Sports*

 I'm a Pro

http://www.nba.com
http://www.nfl.com
http://www.nhl.com
http://www.mlb.com

These are the official sites for the NBA, NFL, NHL, and Major League Baseball. Have a ball!

 The Sporting Life

http://www.cnnsi.com
http://www.sportsline.com
http://www.foxsports.com
http://www.espn.com

If you enjoy sports, do not miss out on these sites.

795 Stop at This Terminal

http://www.sportsterminal.com

Design your own personalized Web page that has all your team favorites. You'll hit this site many times.

796 Sports Search

http://www.sportsearch.com
http://www.sportssleuth.com

If you love sports, search to your heart's content.

797 Sports Network

http://www.sportsnetwork.com

Most sports are covered here, and you can view live scoreboards for many of them.

798 It's a Hit

http://www.sporthits.com

Here's a great site to get directly to the major sports fast.

799 The Best of . . .

http://www.baseball-links.com
http://www.nflfans.com
http://www.nationwide.net/~patricia
http://www.inthecrease.com
http://www.golfonline.com

. . . baseball, football, basketball, hockey, and golf can be found here.

800 I'm the Greatest

http://jordan.sportsline.com
http://www.payton34.com
http://www.2131.com

Jordan, Payton, and Ripken are three of the all-time greats in their respective sports.

801 Legends

http://www.cmgww.com

This site brings you face-to-face with many of the greatest names in sports.

802 College Sports

http://www.fansonly.com

If you enjoy college sports, this site was designed for you.

803 Go, Fight, Win

http://www.1122productions.com/fightsongs

Rah, rah! The fight songs for many colleges are provided here.

804 Sports History

http://www.hickoksports.com/history.shtml

Tradition! Without our sports history, we have no foundation. There's lots of interesting stuff here for us old folks.

805 Traveling Sports Fanatic

http://www.cs.rochester.edu/u/ferguson/schedules
http://www.cs.rochester.edu/u/ferguson/schedules/cities.html

Select a city and a date to find out what sporting event is taking place.

806 Yogi-isms

http://www.yogi-berra.com

It ain't baseball without Yogi-isms!

807 Baseball Fanatics

http://www.baseball-reference.com

If you love baseball, go to this site. It has statistics and records and can help settle a few friendly bets.

808 Pro Stats

http://baseball.ibi.com

Get your stats for baseball, football, basketball, and hockey here.

809 National Pastime

http://www.baseball-almanac.com

Enjoy baseball history, awards, records, humor, feats, lists, quotations, and stats at this site.

810 Who's on First?

http://www.abbottandcostello.net

I don't know!

811 Youth Hockey

http://yhn.eteamz.com

Hockey is a major sport for kids. This site will fill you in about kids on ice.

812 Little League Baseball

http://www.littleleague.org

Apple pie, Mom, and Little League Baseball are the all-American staples.

813 Our Team

http://www.myteam.com

If you've got kids, you're probably very involved with several sports. You can use this site to schedule and communicate with your team members.

814 Youth Sports on the Net

http://www.infosprts.com

Okay kids, find out what is happening on the Net when it comes to sports.

815 I Wanna Be

http://www.tigerwoods.com

It seems like all kids (and adults) want to be Tiger Woods. Visit his official site.

816 GolfWeb

http://www.golfweb.com

GolfWeb has an excellent golf site. If you are a golfer, go here right now.

817 Golf Search

http://www.golfsearch.com

Sorry, this site will not find your lost ball, but it will tell you where to find golf-related items on the Net.

818 It's the Equipment

http://www.golfweb.com/equipment/proreport/index.html

Golfers love getting new clubs. Before you buy your next set, find out what the winning pros are using. See you on the tour.

819 Sports Stadium and Arena Sites

http://www.wwcd.com/stadiums.html
http://www.ballparks.com

If you are a sports fanatic, check out these arena layouts and seating charts.

820 This Stuff Kicks

http://www.mlsnet.com

Soccer has taken the USA by storm. This is Major League Soccer's official site.

821 Float Like a Butterfly . . .

http://www.definitionofchamp.com
http://www.courier-journal.com/ali

"I am the greatest!" Guess who?

822 Be in the Zone

http://www.wrestlezone.com

This site's slogan is "Give me wrestling or give me death." Yes, the Internet does have something for everyone.

823 It's Official

http://www.wwf.com
http://www.wcwwrestling.com

Visit the official sites for these professional sports entertainment giants.

Have a Ball

http://www.justballs.com

The Ball Authority provides sections devoted to buying guides, game rules, ball care, and a Ball Encyclopedia.

>> Stocks & Investments

 ### I Hate Financial Planning

http://www.ihatefinancialplanning.com

You might hate it, but it's a good idea to do some. Make sure you sign up for the weekly planning tip.

 ### Money Central

http://moneycentral.msn.com

Money is central to our lives. This is Microsoft's award-winning site that will help with all aspects of your financial life.

Finance Center

http://www.financenter.com

This excellent site will assist you with credit card, automobile, and home financing issues. Calculators are provided to help make financial decisions.

 ### The Motley Fool

http://www.fool.com

These guys are famous. Their slogan is: "Educate, amuse, enrich." They do all of that and more.

Give Peace a Chance

http://www.financialpeace.com

If you are committed to becoming financially secure, listen to Dave Ramsey's daily radio broadcast.

 ### You Look Like a Million

http://www.armchairmillionaire.com

A million bucks just ain't what it used to be, but it's still not bad. Get simple and practical advice here.

 ### The Stock Market

http://www.nyse.com
http://www.nasdaq.com
http://www.amex.com

All of the major stock markets are here for you.

 ### The Dow Jones Industrial Average

http://www.site-by-site.com/usa/dj.htm
http://www.dogsofthedow.com

Who are the companies that make up the famous index? Read all about an interesting investment strategy at Dogs of the Dow.

Money Makes the World Go 'Round

http://www.cnnfn.com
http://www.cnbc.com
http://cbs.marketwatch.com
http://www.thestreet.com
http://www.on24.com
http://www.money.net

Are you addicted to stock reporting? Let these sites link you to timely news, the markets, opinions, and advice.

834 Hoovers

http://www.hoovers.com

This site proclaims itself as "The ultimate source for company information on the Net."

835 Investing.com

http://www.investormap.com
http://www.investorlinks.com
http://www.investorguide.com

Are you an investor? These guides will make your financial journey very pleasant.

836 Investorama

http://www.investorwords.com
http://www.investorama.com

You'll find thousands of words and thousands of sites here.

837 Portfolio Portal

http://www.dailystocks.com
http://www.justquotes.com
http://www.123jump.com

Enter a stock symbol and you'll receive detailed information about all aspects of that company.

838 NewsAlert

http://www.newsalert.com

This site provides you with news, information, SEC filings, stock quotes, and other information. You can even download a very fine stock ticker.

839 **Yahoo! for Quotes**

http://quote.yahoo.com
http://chart.yahoo.com/d

If you want to track your stocks, Yahoo! will be happy to help. If you need to chart a historical quote, Yahoo! has that information, too.

840 **Savvy Tools**

http://www.bigcharts.com
http://www.bestcalls.com
http://www.earningswhispers.com

Every savvy investor can use the charts, listen to conference calls, and follow the earnings whisper numbers here. Be savvy, use these sites.

841 **Real-Time Quotes**

http://www.ragingbull.com
http://www.freerealtime.com

No delays here, get real-time stock quotes.

842 **Investor's Chat**

http://www.investorschat.com
http://www.investingonline.org

Investment chat rooms and online investing have become unbelievably popular. Test these sites out to see if online investing is your cup of tea.

843 **Message Boards**

http://www.boardcentral.com

You'll never be bored here. This site has message boards, news, company profiles, research, charts, and much more from dozens of leading Web sites.

844 IPO ABCs

http://www.ipocentral.com
http://www.ipodata.com
http://www.edgar-online.com/ipoexpress

If you are interested in initial public offerings, you can become a maven by using these sites.

845 Mutual Funds

http://www.mfea.com
http://www.morningstar.com
http://www.money.com/money/fundcenter

On the Net, these are your guides to mutual funds.

846 Fund Alert

http://www.maxfunds.com
http://www.fundalarm.com
http://www.fundsinteractive.com

The easiest way to get into the market is through mutual funds. Let these sites help you become a knowledgeable investor.

847 U.S. Savings Bonds

http://www.savingsbonds.gov

This site has a lot of information, but the best is the bond calculator. If you have any federal bonds, go here to find out their current value.

848 Be an Insider

http://www.insidertrader.com
http://www.individualinvestor.com

Pop in a stock symbol and identify the insiders who own that stock.

849   Get Serious

http://www.thomsoninvest.net
http://www.multexinvestor.com

Here are research sites for the serious investor.

850   Let's Get Technical

http://www.clearstation.com

This site claims to be "for the intelligent investment community."

851   World Economy

http://www.worldlyinvestor.com

We're in a world economy, so here's a site dedicated to international investing.

852   Get in the League

http://www.investorsleague.com

Get $100,000 worth of play money to invest in the stock market. This stock market simulator is from the League of American Investors. It offers one of the most effective methods to learn about investing.

853   It's Only a Game

http://www.smg2000.org

The Stock Market Game lets participants discover the risks and rewards involved in decision-making, the sources and uses of capital, and other related economic concepts.

Play the Market

>http://www.marketplayer.com
>http://www.marketguide.com

>Build and test your own stock market strategy. For assistance while playing the market, see the guide.

 Let's Trade

>http://www.gomez.com
>http://www.eschwab.com
>http://www.etrade.com

>Let Gomez and others assist you when it comes to trading stocks via the Net.

 Purchase One Share of Stock

>http://www.oneshare.com

>This is not intended to be your place to trade stocks on the Internet. Its purpose is for gift items. For example, some of the hottest sellers are Apple Computer and the Boston Celtics.

 Stock Direct

>http://www.netstockdirect.com

>Now, you can buy stocks directly from companies. Yes, that is correct—no broker commissions.

>> *Teachers*

 Teacher's Resource

>http://www.pbs.org/teachersource
>http://www.teachersfirst.com

>Though these sites are primarily designed for teachers, we can all learn things from them.

859 Lesson Plans

http://encarta.msn.com/schoolhouse
http://www.homeworkcentral.com/teachers
http://www.nytimes.com/learning/teachers/lessons

Thousands of lesson plans for every subject can be found at these sites designed for the educator.

860 Teachers' Journals

http://www.thejournal.com
http://www.education-world.com

These sites are designed to assist teachers with the Internet.

861 Web Treasures for Teachers

http://www.classroom.com/edsoasis
http://www.connectedteacher.com/library/bestofweb.asp

These sites are organized by school subject area, and you will find a few treasures here. These are also good sites to show to your students.

862 Educational Quizzes

http://www.quia.com

Quia provides a directory of thousands of online games and quizzes in more than forty subject areas. You can even create your own online quizzes.

863 CyberBee

http://www.cyberbee.com

From great clip art to other excellent educational sites on the Web, Linda (the bee) has them for you.

Kathy Schrock

http://discoveryschool.com/schrockguide

Kathy has a simple and informative page for kids, teachers, and parents.

>> *Technology*

There are No Dumb Questions

http://answers.dummies.com

Where can I find fun and straightforward answers to my technology questions? The answer is here.

Be a Maven

http://www.businessweek.com/technology/list/flash01.htm

Business Week knows computers and technology, offering its computer buying guide and articles from its "Technology & You" column.

Living with Technology

http://www.technocopia.com

Is technology taking over your life? This interesting site discusses its effects at home, work, and play.

High Tech Sites

http://www.techsightings.com

Get reviews of the best high-tech sites on the Net.

Best of What's New

http://www.popsci.com/features/bown/bown99
http://www.popsci.com/features/bown/bown00

This *Popular Science* site lists the one hundred best achievements in science and technology.

 ### The New Economy

http://www.wired.com
http://www.upside.com
http://www.business2.com
http://www.redherring.com
http://www.fastcompany.com

These magazines offer help in understanding today's business and technology.

The Internet Economy

http://www.thestandard.com
http://www.hotwired.com
http://www.interactiveweek.com

Are you fascinated by the stocks, technology, and growth of the Internet economy? These sites will keep you I-informed.

"I tapped into the school's computer and changed all my grades. Then the school tapped into my computer and changed all my games to educational programs!"

>> *Teens*

872 **Teen Voices**

http://www.teenvoices.com
http://www.teen.com
http://www.teenrefuge.com

Here are great places for teenagers to hang out.

873 **Teens Online**

http://www.bolt.com

Everything teenagers discuss is here—well, almost everything.

874 **Cyberteens**

http://www.cyberkids.com
http://www.cyberteens.com

Here's an online community for young people from all over the world who share their thoughts and ideas with each other.

875 **Pop Goes the . . .**

http://www.pimpleportal.com

. . . pimple! You've got to love a site that is dedicated to a teen's worst nightmare.

>> Telephony

876 Ye Old Telephone

http://www.museumphones.com

Visit the Cyber Telephone Museum here to learn about the origins and evolution of this important communication device.

877 Let's Talk

http://www.vocaltec.com

http://www.pulver.com/fwd

The Net offers free telephone calls to locations all over the world.

878 Long Distance for Free

http://www.dialpad.com

http://www.net2phone.com

Sign up with these services, and you can make long-distance calls for free on the Net. You can even reach out and touch someone who is not on the Internet.

879 Phone Home

http://phone.yahoo.com

http://anywhere.lycos.com

For those who want to stay connected, Yahoo! and Lycos offer voice mail, e-mail, and Web content all via the phone.

880 Ring, Ring, Ring

http://www.mrwakeup.com

http://www.tellme.com

With wake-up calls, daily reminders, stock market updates, and more, this service will call you with the information you request.

>> *Television*

881 **Your Guide to TV**

http://www.tvguide.com
http://www.tvgrid.com
http://www.clicktv.com

Yes, you can get your *TV Guide* online.

882 **Click This**

http://tv.zap2it.com

Get zapped into the world of TV news, shows, people, and more. Just click it.

883 **I Like TV**

http://www.liketelevision.com

Take a trip down memory lane. Watch Burns and Allen, The Lone Ranger, classic movies, and more.

884 **Episode Guide**

http://www.epguides.com

This site contains episode lists for over 1600 TV shows. Each list contains titles and airdates. For over 375 shows there is a more detailed episode guide containing guest stars and plot summaries.

885 **David Letterman**

http://www.cbs.com/latenight/lateshow

Did you miss David's monologue last night? Hear ye, hear ye, it's on the Net.

886 10, 9, 8 . . . 1

http://marketing.cbs.com/lateshow/topten/archive

David Letterman's Top Ten lists have become legend. Now you can read them all the way back to 1993.

887 Comedy Central

http://www.comedycentral.com

It doesn't get much funnier than this. Visit the home of Jon Stewart's *Daily Show*, *South Park* and other shows.

888 TV Women Love

http://www.oprah.com
http://www.rosie.com

Oprah and Rosie address your interests, loves, concerns, and deepest worries. They are smart, sassy, funny, serious, spiritual, and inspirational.

889 Nickelodeon on the Net

http://www.nick.com

Nick is fun on TV and on the Net, too.

890 Going Looney

http://www.nonstick.com

You'll go Looney over this site. Hurry up, Bugs and friends aren't going to wait.

891 Fox Kids

http://www.foxkids.com

If you like the Fox TV shows, check out the fun they have in store for you.

PBS

http://www.pbs.org

If you enjoy the high-quality programming on PBS, then no doubt you will enjoy PBS Online. If you want a weekly update, get on the e-mail update list.

Let's Get Critical

http://www.adcritic.com

Love 'em or hate 'em, we all discuss TV commercials, and AdCritic has everything about the old, the new, and the best.

>> Toys & Collectibles

Toy Time!

http://www.toysrus.com
http://www.faoschwarz.com

Everyone's a kid at FAO Schwarz and Toys R Us.

Dr. Toy

http://www.drtoy.com

Over one thousand award-winning toys and various children's products are selected and fully described by Dr. Toy, with company phone numbers so you can call for more information.

Internet Collectible Awards

http://www.collectiblenet.com

This site selects some of the best collectible sites on the Net. From antiques to trading cards, you'll find a great collection.

897 Beanie Babies

http://www.ty.com
http://www.beaniemom.com
http://www.absolutebeanies.com

Check out a complete listing and biography of all these critters.

898 The Latest Craze

http://www.pokemon.com
http://www.pokemontop50.com

It's colorful, and it's unbelievably popular with kids. If you have no idea what Pokémon is, visit here to find out. And if you're a collector, indulge your passion at these sites.

899 Fads Online

http://www.bandai.com

From Power Rangers to dinosaurs, Bandai has 'em for you.

900 Crayola

http://www.crayola.com

Binney and Smith help us be kids. Now, get to the coloring!

901 Sanrio

http://www.sanrio.com

If you know Hello Kitty, Keroppi, or Pochacco, you must visit them on the Net. Of course, there are lots more friends waiting for you.

>> *Travel*

902 **Travel Portal**

http://www.johnnyjet.com

Take a trip to Johnny's site, and you will be rewarded with everything you ever needed to know about travel on the Internet.

903 **Travel Hits the Spot**

http://www.tripspot.com

This travel portal surfs the Web to help identify the very best travel sites. You'll also find insightful editorial content.

904 **Travel Search Engine**

http://www.kasbah.com

As you plan your next trip, make sure you visit here for travel directories and search engines.

905 **Book It Here**

http://expedia.msn.com
http://www.travelocity.com

Preview these award-winning sites before you travel anywhere.

906 **Trip.com**

http://www.trip.com

Track airline flights and view hotel, restaurant, and weather information for particular cities.

907   Business Traveler

http://www.biztravel.com

You can track flights in progress, learn about cities throughout the world, get directions, obtain your frequent flyer miles (from some airlines) and more.

908   May I Help You?

http://www.concierge.com

When traveling, this concierge can be your best guide to a city.

909   Travel Source

http://www.msnbc.com/Modules/Travel/toolkit.asp
http://www.travelsource.com

Are you a serious traveler? If so, then don't leave home without these sites.

910   Guide Me, Please

http://www.frommers.com
http://www.fodors.com

You don't want to go anywhere without consulting these award-winning online publications.

911   It's a *Rough* World

http://travel.roughguides.com

With information on over four thousand destinations, you are bound to find some great places for traveling. The *Rough Guides'* site helps you find out about lodging, dining, and entertainment.

912   Your Travel Guide

http://www.mytravelguide.com

Make this portal site one of your destinations for travel plans.

913 All the Hotels on the Web

http://www.all-hotels.com

http://www.hotelguide.com

There's over sixty thousand of them. Sleep tight.

914 Auto Rentals

http://www.bnm.com

Here's your guide to over ninety major auto rental companies at more than one hundred airports. Drive safely!

915 Chase a Deal

http://www.farechase.com

http://www.qixo.com

Streamline the process of searching for good travel deals by comparing real-time fare quotes culled from more than a dozen sites.

916 Flyin' Cheap

http://www.priceline.com

http://www.hotwire.com

Go to these sites and tell these folks what you are willing to pay for a plane ticket. You just might get a great airfare.

917 The Best and Lowest Fares

http://www.bestfares.com

http://www.lowestfare.com

http://www.lowairfare.com

http://www.air-fare.com

http://www.cheaptickets.com

Get the best possible prices on plane tickets by using these sites.

918 FAA Online

http://www.faa.gov

The Federal Aviation Agency is required to provide safety records and other pertinent information about airlines at its Web site.

919 Going Local

http://local.yahoo.com
http://travel.lycos.com
http://www.citysearch.com
http://www.digitalcity.com

These sites have a lot of information about cities. If you are traveling, require information about a town, or just want to know, dive right in.

920 CNN City Guides

http://www.cnn.com/travel

Get a map of just about any city in the world. You can also obtain specific details about many cities.

921 Only the Best

http://www.10best.com

10Best simplifies your search for the best by listing accurate and comprehensive destination details for everything there is to do in a city.

922 Location, Location, Location

http://www.bestplaces.net

This site can help you choose the best places to live, work, play, or retire.

923 Cities A to Z

http://www.expedia.com/wg/P36380.asp

Click on a city, and you will find information about it.

924 The Big Apple

http://www.nycvisit.com

This is the official tourism Web site of the New York Convention & Visitors Bureau.

925 The Greatest Places

http://www.greatestplaces.org

Here are seven places you might never have a chance to visit: the Amazon, Greenland, Tibet, Iguazu, Madagascar, Okavango, and Namib. Check them out online.

926 What's Your Orientation?

http://www.orientation.com

Here's a great portal site that focuses on detailed information from six continents. Sorry, North America is not included.

927 Travel Q&A

http://www.geocities.com/TheTropics/2442/database.html

Got travel questions? Arranged by geographic location, this is a database of people throughout the world who have the answers.

928 Ticked Off

http://www.ticked.com
http://www.passengerrights.com

Here is clean, credible, cutting edge travel advice for "the ticked-off tourist."

929 Road Construction

http://www.randmcnally.com

Before you head off on that next road trip, check this site out to see if there is any construction going on along the way. There are also many other interesting sites to see while touring this one.

930 Slow Down!

http://www.speedtrap.com

Nobody likes getting a speeding ticket. Before you go on the road, check out this site to learn where the speed traps are.

931 Get Your Kicks

http://www.route66.com

Ever miss the good old days—before Interstate Highways? Go cruisin' down Route 66.

932 Roadside America

http://www.roadsideamerica.com
http://www.roadsidepeek.com

These sites are your online guides to some offbeat tourist attractions.

933 Traveling to a Foreign Country?

http://www.travlang.com

This site has a lot of valuable information about foreign travel. It also has a translation section that is quite interesting.

934 Currency Converter

http://www.x-rates.com
http://www.oanda.com

These are easy-to-use currency conversion sites. If you're heading out of the country, or are just plain curious, check them out.

>> *Trivia, Quizzes & Tests*

 Get a Fix

http://www.dailyfix.com

http://www.uselessknowledge.com

Each day of the week, go here to get a new quote, piece of trivia, and something to make you smile.

 Curious?

http://www.didyouknow.com

http://www.factcat.com

Do you ask a lot of questions? Check out these sites for a lot of answers.

 Trivia on the Net

http://www.funtrivia.com

http://www.triviabytes.com

http://www.triviaworld.com

Find such trivia as: "What famous comedian was once fined $10,000 for smuggling—Bob Hope, Jimmy Durante, Jack Benny, or George Burns?"

 Absolutely Trivia

http://www.trivia.net

http://www.absolutetrivia.com

If you are a trivia fan, check out these sites. There are thousands of questions.

 Ray's Trivia Page

http://www.primate.wisc.edu/people/hamel/trivia.html

If it has to do with trivia, Ray knows about it.

940 Who Wants to Be a . . .

http://abc.go.com/primetime/millionaire

. . . millionaire?

941 Take the Challenge

http://www.quizland.com

Land at Quizland, and you'll enjoy the quizzes, puzzles, and trivia.

942 High Q

http://www.test.com

Okay, take these tests and show everyone how smart you are.

943 Did You Know?

http://www.triviaspot.com

Spend some time here to learn an interesting fact or piece of trivia.

944 Twenty Questions

http://www.20q.net

Remember the game Twenty Questions? In this version, the computer asks the questions in an attempt to guess what you are thinking. I finally gave up after it beat me twice!

945 It's a Fact

http://features.learningkingdom.com/fact/archive

Peruse these archives of interesting facts. They're guaranteed to make you feel more knowledgeable.

>> *Weather*

946 **Weather Fans**

http://www.weather.com
http://www.wunderground.com

It's everyone's favorite topic of conversation, and with these sites, you won't be left out in the cold.

947 **The Weather Plan . . .**

http://www.weatherplanner.com
http://inbox.weather.com
http://www.intellicast.com

. . . is here for the weather fan.

948 **Historical Weather**

http://www.weatherpost.com/historical/historical.htm

The temperature and precipitation data for over two thousand cities worldwide is available in this complete historical database.

949 **Get the Bug**

http://www.weatherbug.com

Download this weather utility; you'll always know the temperature, and you'll also receive extreme weather alerts.

950 **Weather Cam**

http://cirrus.sprl.umich.edu/wxnet/wxcam.html

What's the weather look like in Alaska? How about Hawaii? You'll be able to watch the weather in every state in the U.S. and Canada, too.

951 Hurricane Season

http://www.nhc.noaa.gov
http://www.gopbi.com/weather/special/storm

From Adam to Zoie, you can watch, listen, and learn about any storm that is brewing.

952 Weird Weather

http://www.owl.on.ca/ww

Weather can be strange. This entertaining site will inform you about a lot of weird weather throughout the world.

"If we really want business to improve, we need to get our own Web page on the Internet!"

>> Web Site

953 Dot Com

http://www.startstorm.com
http://www.networksolutions.com

Is the domain name (Web address) you want still available? This site will let you know. If you have not yet reserved the name, click on over to Network Solutions and get it registered for a small fee.

954 Let Freedomain Reign

http://www.domainzero.com

Register for a free domain name here and have it routed to one of those very long Web addresses that you have.

Join a Community

http://www.tripod.com

http://www.geocities.com

Create your own Web page, join a community, and find lots of other goodies at these sites. Even if you are not creating a site at this time, make sure you check these communities out.

 ## Simple Web Address

http://this.is

http://surf.to

If you want to simplify or customize the address (URL) of your Web site, go here. By the way, the people who provide these services are located in Iceland and Tonga, respectively.

 ## Student Sites

http://www.thinkquest.org

There's a lot of talk today about the poor education our children are getting. Go to this site for a different view.

 ## Free Web Site

http://www.beseen.com

http://www.pagetalk.com

http://www.netfreebies.net

http://www.freesitetools.com

You can use these sites to add many professional utilities to your Web site for free. Don't dare pass these up.

 ## Online Customer Service

http://www.humanclick.com

Click on over to this site and you'll be able to offer interactive customer service at your own site. Best of all, this service is free.

960 ## Your Web Page

http://www.yahoo.com/docs/yahootogo/index.html
http://websitegarage.netscape.com

Yahootogo lets you place some good stuff on your Web page—a search engine, the weather, maps and more. Then, go for a Web site checkup at the garage.

961 ## Gizmos

http://www.gizmoznetworks.com

One of the best designed sites on the Net, Gizmoz allows you to place interactive, animated objects on your Web site or in your e-mail.

962 ## My Own Store

http://store.yahoo.com

Need a Web site for your business? If you want one that requires a storefront and the ability to handle credit card transactions, here is a quick, easy, and inexpensive way to get started.

963 ## Web Pages Simplified

http://www.lissaexplains.com

Lissa, a teenager, explains in clear terminology how to design a Web site.

964 ## Poor Richard

http://www.poorrichard.com

Poor Richard wants you to know everything about having a Web site. His site is rich with many links to assist you.

Ralph's Web

http://www.wilsonweb.com

Ralph Wilson has been out there educating people about creating and marketing Web sites for years. Go ahead, sign up for his free newsletter.

 Marketing on the Net

http://www.wdfm.com

Each week, Larry Chase will send you a newsletter that has fifteen marketing-oriented Web sites. At his Web site, you can review his newsletter archives.

 Ask Dr. Web

http://www.zeldman.com/faq4f.html

Dr. Web wants you to have a well-designed site. He offers some very candid and thought-provoking suggestions on how to make a Web site all it can be.

 The Megalist

http://www.mmgco.com/top100.html
http://www.2020tech.com/submit.html
http://www.submit-it.com

Here are some sites that should help identify places that will list your Web site.

"My husband passed away eight months ago, but we still keep in touch. His e-mail address is WalterZ@Heaven.com."

>> Weird & Wacky

 969 **It's a Record**

http://www.guinnessworldrecords.com

Guinness is world renowned for weird, strange, and unbelievable records.

970 **New York's Underground**

http://www.nationalgeographic.com/features/97/nyunderground

Want to know what's happening in the underbelly of New York? National Geographic gives you a tour of New York's underground, an area that no tour guide will show you.

971 **Darwin Awards**

http://www.darwinawards.com

Recognized posthumously, these award winners have done some strange things and have not lived to talk about them.

972 **Internet Mania**

http://www.dotcomscoop.com
http://www.thecompost.com
http://www.itulip.com

The Internet will change the world, however, some people have gone overboard. These sites highlight some of the dotcom issues.

973 Strange Headlines

http://www.3bp.com

Stop here for a few moments and view a collection of funny and odd headlines and photos.

974 Weird News

http://www.newsoftheweird.com

Here's proof that true stories are weirder than made-up stories.

975 Documents

http://www.thesmokinggun.com

The Smoking Gun is well-known for obtaining and publishing documents that are public record. Some of these documents are interesting in relation to current events and for historical purposes.

976 The Skeptic's Dictionary

http://www.skepdic.com

From A to Z, this skeptic has some definitions and additional resources to study.

977 Seconds to Live

http://www.deathclock.com

How much time do you have left? This unique site estimates your life span and shows it to you as a timer counting down the seconds. You can even make this your screensaver.

978 Dream On

http://www.swoon.com/dream

Do you ever remember your dreams? Curious about what they might mean? This site will help interpret what you experienced.

979 **Disinformation, Please**

http://www.disinfo.com

We live in a world of disinformation. Find out about all that bad info here.

980 **Let's Get Nutty, Buddy**

http://www.nuttysites.com

This site is dedicated to promoting the awareness of entertaining, clever, funny, and plain old nutty Web sites.

981 **Fighting Ignorance . . .**

http://www.straightdope.com

. . . since 1973, Cecil Adams—self-proclaimed World's Smartest Human Being—provides "all worthwhile human knowledge" on a variety of topics.

982 **License Plates of the World**

http://danshiki.oit.gatech.edu/~iadt3mk/index.html

Ever play the game of looking for different state license plates when traveling? This site has them from all over the world.

983 **Isn't Life Strange?**

http://www.theweirdsite.com

People and the Internet can both be very bizarre. Check out some of these odd things at this site.

984 **This is Stupid!**

http://www.dumblaws.com

In my hometown, it is illegal to spit from a car or bus, but citizens may do so from a truck. Check out dumb laws in your area.

985 Urban Legend Has It . . .

http://www.snopes.com
http://www.urbanlegends.com

. . . that most of these stories are actually untrue! Legends spread even faster on the Net, but these sites might help debunk a few for you.

986 Casper the Friendly Ghost

http://www.ghosts.org/links.html

Yes, there are ghosts even in cyberspace. This site has a lot of spooky stuff.

987 When the Sky Fell

http://www.disasterium.com

At the Living Almanac of Disasters, click on any day of the yearly calendar and see what calamities occurred on that date in history. You can even do a separate search for fires, earthquakes, and major transportation catastrophes.

988 Spoof It Up

http://www.theonion.com
http://www.wackytimes.com

With all the bad news floating around the world, we need more sites like these. They are guaranteed to make you laugh.

989 Off the Wall

http://www.nationallampoon.com

It's fun, it's goofy, it's spoofy, and totally graphic. Sit back, relax, and don't fall off your chair while laughing.

990 Letters from Bill

http://www.cranial.com/hertes.html

William Hertes has an interesting hobby. He sends odd letters to corporations, and these companies usually reply. At this site, Bill shares some of these hilarious letters with us.

991 Rules are Made to Be Broken

http://www.everyrule.com

Without rules, we have no order. You'll find rules for sports, games, and much more here.

>> Women

992 It Takes a Village

http://www.ivillage.com
http://www.women.com
http://www.oxygen.com

These villages are designed for women. From beauty to working at home, you'll find it all here.

993 Women in the News

http://www.womensenews.org

The stated goal of Women's Enews is to provide a professional news service to the public and the media, policy makers and opinion shapers, covering the news about issues of importance to women.

994 Join the Forum

http://www.womensforum.com

This grassroots portal was developed to profile women's sites, leading you to over a hundred sites of interest.

It's a Woman Thing

http://www.herplanet.com

This planet is all about women, and it's made up of many Web sites that address issues for home life, business, and the Internet. You'll even find a section on "Women to Watch."

 ### Cancer Awareness

http://www.nationalbreastcancer.org
http://www.thebreastclinic.com
http://www.cancerhelp.com
http://www.findcancerexperts.com

Being informed is half the battle. Explore—don't ignore—this major threat to women.

>> Writing & Writers

 ### Pens and Pencils

http://www.parkerpen.co.uk/history
http://www.pencils.com

We use them all the time. Now you can learn just about everything you ever needed to know about pens and pencils.

 ### Young Writer

http://www.writing-world.com
http://www.writersdigest.com
http://bookbarn.odsys.net/childmkt

If you have the writing bug, these writers will educate and motivate you. You're never too young or too old to become a writer.

Samuel Langhorne Clemens

http://library.berkeley.edu/BANC/MTP

If you don't know who he is, then you need to visit this site. Tom and Huck are waiting for you.

>> **Zoos**

 ### Zoo Mania

http://www.zooweb.com
http://www.beyondzoo.org
http://netvet.wustl.edu/e-zoo.htm

Visit these sites to find out all about zoos and animals on the Net.

 ### Zoos and Aquariums

http://www.aza.org

If you need to find a zoo or aquarium in North America, this association has it listed.

◀ Index of Site Numbers ▶

T

U

V

W

❮ The Incredible Newsletter ❯

If you are enjoying this book, you can also arrange to receive a steady stream of more "incredible Internet things" delivered directly to your e-mail address.

The Leebow Letter, Ken Leebow's weekly e-mail newsletter, provides new sites, updates on existing ones, and information about other happenings on the Internet.

For more details about *The Leebow Letter* and how to subscribe, visit us at: WWW.300INCREDIBLE.COM

❮ United Service Organizations (USO) ❯

For nearly sixty years, the United Service Organizations (USO) has "Delivered America" to service members stationed around the world, thousands of miles from family and friends. The USO provides celebrity entertainment, recreation, cultural orientation, language training, travel assistance, telephone and Internet access, and other vital services to military personnel and their families at 115 locations worldwide. The USO is a nonprofit organization, not a government agency. It relies on the generosity of corporations and individuals to enable its programs and services to continue. For more information on contributing to the USO, please call 1-800-876-7469 or visit its Web site at www.uso.org.

❮ About the Author ❯

KEN LEEBOW has been involved in the computer business for over twenty years. The Internet has fascinated him since he began exploring it several years ago, and he has helped over a million readers utilize its resources. Ken has appeared frequently in the media, educating individuals about the Web's greatest hits. He is considered a leading expert on what is incredible about the Internet.

When he is not online, you can find Ken playing tennis, golf, running, reading, or spending time with his family. He is living proof that being addicted to the Net doesn't mean giving up on the other pleasures of life.

❮ Notes ❯

❮ Notes ❯

❮ Notes ❯

❮ Notes ❯

❮ Notes ❯